A Sporting Chance

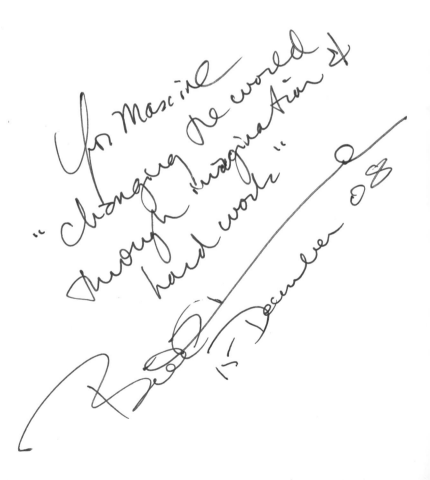

For Massine

"changing the world through imagination et hard work"

Best December '08

A SPORTING CHANCE

Achievements of
African-Canadian Athletes

WILLIAM HUMBER

Foreword by Spider Jones

NATURAL HERITAGE BOOKS
TORONTO

Published by Natural Heritage / Natural History Inc.
P.O. Box 95, Station O, Toronto, On M4A 2M8
www.naturalheritagebooks.com

All photographs are courtesy of the author unless otherwise identified.
Front cover, *clockwise from top left:* Perdita Felicien, *Courtesy of the University of Illinois Sports Information*; Jarome Iginla, *Courtesy of the Hockey Hall of Fame*; Larry Gains, *Courtesy of Canada's Sports Hall of Fame*; Rosella Thorne, *Courtesy of Canada's Sports Hall of Fame.*
Back cover, *clockwise from top right:* Patrick Husbands winning the Queen's Plate, *Courtesy of Woodbine Entertainment*, Fergie Jenkins, *Courtesy of Leo Kelly*; Perdita Felicien, *Courtesy of Nike Canada Ltd.*; Herb Carnegie, *Courtesy of the Carnegie Family Collection*; Molly Killingbeck, *Courtesy of Tony Techko.*

Design by Blanche Hamill, Norton Hamill Design
Edited by Catherine Leek
Printed and bound in Canada by Hignell Book Printing, Winnipeg, Manitoba

The text in this book was set in a typeface named Minion.

Library and Archives Canada Cataloguing in Publication

Humber, William, 1949–
    A sporting chance : achievements of African-Canadian athletes / William Humber ; foreword by Spider Jones.

Includes bibliographical references and index.
ISBN 1-896219-99-3

    1. Athletes, Black—Canada. 2. Discrimination in sports—Canada. 3. Racism in sports—Canada. I. Title.

GV697.A1H84 2004   796'.089'96071   C2004-905750-2

Canada 🍁

ONTARIO ARTS COUNCIL
CONSEIL DES ARTS DE L'ONTARIO

THE CANADA COUNCIL | LE CONSEIL DES ARTS
FOR THE ARTS | DU CANADA
SINCE 1957 | DEPUIS 1957

Natural Heritage / Natural History Inc. acknowledges the financial support of the Canada Council for the Arts and the Ontario Arts Council for our publishing program. We acknowledge the support of the Government of Ontario through the Ontario Media Development Corporation's Ontario Book Initiative. We also acknowledge the financial support of the Government of Canada through the Book Publishing Industry Development Program (BPIDP) and the Association for the Export of Canadian Books.

Contents

Acknowledgements

A history is more than a simple record of the past. It attempts to broaden our understanding of both another time and of our own.

My interest in the sporting achievements of African-Canadian athletes dates back to my research on Canada's baseball, cycling and Olympic history. I continually discovered that the isolation of many minorities, and in particular that of Black athletes, from the sporting mainstream was not limited to the United States but played a significant role in Canada's development.

In the process I hope to open a window on the Canadian experience of some of its first citizens. This includes the years in which the Black population was so small as to be almost invisible, to the impact of immigration and the transformation in Canadian sporting achievement. Today issues surrounding race continue to be part of a larger public dialogue, even as a broader understanding of what it means to be Canadian and the rise of a generation prepared to describe themselves as ethnically ambiguous transcends older and more limited definitions of identity.

Thanks to Barry Penhale and Jane Gibson and their extraordinary staff at Natural Heritage Books for making this book possible. A tip of the hat to Ken Pearson and Sheldon Taylor who reviewed earlier versions of this book, and special regards to my favourite radio personality and long time friend Chuck "Spider" Jones.

Others who provided help included my neighbour Hugh Walters, Tony Techko, members of the BigUp Volleyball organization, Canada's Sports Hall of Fame and its director Alan Stewart, Phil Edwards' daughter Gwen Emery, Ray Lewis, David Crichton, Karen Clarke, E.G. Hastings, Donna Ford, Bill Linton, Melissa Thomas, Ed Grenda, James Duplacey, David

Shury, Kevin Walsh, Renaldo Nehemiah, Woodbine Entertainment, my brother Larry Humber, and many others, including students in my Canadian sports history course at Seneca College.

Appreciation, as always, to my family including Cathie and our children Brad, Darryl and Karen.

I dedicate this book to the almost forgotten Bob Berry, champion rower, barred from competition in a Toronto Regatta, a bare month after Canada became a nation. Let this be a rebuke to the behaviour of small-minded men. Berry was a true Canadian and of that company, as described in Ecclesiastes, whose "bodies are buried in peace but their name liveth for evermore."

Foreword

I've got a high noon hook-up with a publisher who's expressed deep interest in another book I've been working on. The rendezvous is to take place in downtown Toronto and, as usual, the Spider is running late. I check the clock on the kitchen wall as I'm cuttin' out the back door. The big hand's on six and the little one on ten, which allows approximately 30 minutes to make my 40-mile destination. In addition, I'll have to find a parking spot in the heart of downtown Toronto! That's kind of like searching for a wart on Tyra Banks' face.

Just as I slam the door behind me, the phone rings! So it's back inside and dash for the blower. "Hi Spider, it's Bill Humber, you got a few seconds?" P-u-l-e-e-z-e! I'm running so late, a few seconds are like eternity. I'm getting ready to blow him off quicker than heaven gets the news. But before I get the opportunity, he informs me that he's just completed his latest literary venture entitled *A Sporting Chance*…and now all he requires is the introduction I'd promised him.

Say What! An introduction! Sure, I was flattered when he approached me with the idea, but since then I'd taken on so many commitments that it had completely eluded me. Nevertheless, Humber is a special friend and someone who has always been conscientious and supportive in the fight for racial equality. Keeping this in mind, I left him with a promise the intro would be in his possession within a few days. First, I'd have to read the book. When I eventually laid it to rest in the wee hours of the following morning I was infinitely a wiser soul.

As an avid sports fan whose roots are deeply entrenched in Canadian history I can honestly say that *A Sporting Chance* is not only a historical treasure, but also an enlightening revelation into the African-Canadian sports culture. The book is loaded to the gills with countless inspirational stories and anecdotes about our nation's greatest Black athletes. There are, of course, the exploits of Lennox Lewis, Donovan Bailey and Ferguson Jenkins, but also more recent heroes like Jarome Iginla, arguably the best all-round hockey player on the planet. He's a perfect role model for Canadian youth of all cultures. And so is Perdita Felicien from my own community in Pickering, Ontario. She is Canada's premier track and field performer and a world champion with a contagious smile.

Humber tells the stories of other distinguished female athletes like Sylvia Sweeney and Molly Killingbeck both of whom continued to provide leadership after their athletic careers ended. He reminds us of a generation of women who came to Canada as children after immigration's doors were opened. They transformed Canada's track and field identity in the 1980s and beyond.

Their feats have been well-documented in the sporting pages of our major papers. Unfortunately, numerous other great Black Canadian athletes have been grossly ignored, or pardon the pun, blacked out by the media. Perhaps this lack of acknowledgement is because of ignorance, bias or short-sightedness, which has grossly afflicted too many of our nation's journalists. This is not my time nor book to debate such issues. With his broad knowledge, compassion and courage, Humber has succeeded in doing an admirable job of boldly going where few have dared to tread as he reflects on many of our nation's forgotten athletes. He speaks with passion of their struggles against racism in a country that has long denied its existence.

Spider Jones is one of Canada's most dynamic speakers with a story, now available in his book, *Out of the Darkness* (ECW Press, 2003). He hosts the ESPN Classic Series on boxing with his long-time pal George Chuvalo. Spider can be heard on Canada's premier radio station CFRB where, in honour of his long ago days in the fight game, he seldom pulls his punches.

A Sporting Chance stimulated and resurrected many bygone memories for me, including Earl Walls, George Godfrey, Larry Gains and Clyde Gray, four of the greatest boxers this country has produced. Each was a genuine Hall of Famer. All were revered within Black communities. Yet the distinguished feats of these extraordinary athletes have too often faded into obscurity. Humber's tribute to them conjures sweet memories of their past glory. But it also brings back painful memories of times when racial antagonism turned the dreams of many great African-Canadian athletes into nightmares.

Ever hear of Sam Richardson and Ray Lewis? They were two of Canada's first great track stars. Long before Ben Johnson and Donovan Bailey emerged, these track and field pioneers experienced the foul winds of racism. Yet through it all they rolled with the punches of persecution, and they proudly carried the spirit of our nation into Olympic action. Valerie Jerome was another gifted competitor who toiled in obscurity at a time when female athletes of any colour were generally ignored.

Back in the late 1940s and early fifties, Fred Thomas was Windsor, Ontario's, most beloved hero. Sadly, his is another tale of an extraordinary Black athlete whose road to glory was barricaded by racism. Thomas excelled in many sports including basketball. If not for the racial barriers of the day he would have been fast-tracked to the major leagues of several sports. In 1949 the Toronto *Globe and Mail* called him, "The best Negro athlete in Canada." Their accolade fell short, however, for he was likely the best athlete, period.

Herb Carnegie is another story of broken dreams. Back in the 1950s he was a smooth skater and electrifying forward in Quebec's elite professional league. Unfortunately some years before, Conn Smythe, owner of the Toronto Maple Leafs, was said to have rhetorically quipped that he'd pay anyone $10,000 if they could turn Carnegie white.

In this compelling book, Humber shares additional stories of athletes who suffered because of the social injustices of their day. Names like Robert Berry, a great rower at the time of Confederation, banned from competing in his home town's annual regatta, or Sam Langford, pound-for-pound one of the greatest to lace them up, are now forgotten. Even George Dixon, the first Black man to ever capture a world boxing title seldom gets his due when sports pages exalt our nation's past sports heroes.

A story that particularly evoked memories for me was that of a man whose name popped up in the barbershops and street corners of the Black communities of my youth in Windsor and across the border in Detroit. John Joseph Evans, better known as J.J., excelled in Negro league baseball during the forties. My father, who saw Jackie Robinson, Josh Gibson and Willie Mays, swore that Evans was in their class. He said only the colour barrier kept Evans from the majors.

A Sporting Chance is a revelation. It shares bittersweet tales of the human spirit's victory over insurmountable odds. It's a provocative and inspirational read that stirs both the heart and soul, even as it tells about salt poured into the wounds of racism. *A Sporting Chance* is a hard-hitting, eye-opening experience that had to be written. It's a definite must on the shelves of every library and school across our country. My deepest regard to Bill Humber for the plethora of time and effort he's devoted to this historical gem.

You are the man!

– SPIDER JONES

PART ONE

)

1

THE BLACK EXPERIENCE IN CANADA

FOR THOUSANDS OF YEARS, the land mass we now know as Canada was home to the people of its First Nations. They had crossed into the Western Hemisphere from Asia and created distinctive lives of settled and nomadic character. They developed a multitude of varying tribal organizations, within which evolved unique cultures and languages. Then about 500 years ago a new settlement began. It consisted of white-skinned Europeans and shortly thereafter black-skinned Africans, the former having power and authority, the latter subjugated in positions of imposed servitude.

The first-known Black man to arrive in Canada was Mathieu DaCosta, Champlain's translator with the Mi'Knaw First Nation in 1603. Formal Black residency came later. The experience of Black people in North America is inextricably tied to the long period of slavery in the western world dating back to Europe's great age of discovery beginning in the 15th century. It lasted through first Great Britain's and then America's abolition of the institution in the 19th century. It was followed by a century of legalized segregation, particularly in the United States. Today it is characterized by a continuing pursuit of racial equality. Most of these turbulent events were centred in the United States but Canada's proximity ensured its witness and occasional participation in this greater drama.

Great Britain's absolute authority in its Canadian and American territories of North America was brief, lasting from the Treaty of Paris, under which the French government ceded New France in 1763, and concluding with the American Declaration of Independence in 1776, resulting in the loss of the 13 colonies.

Records in New France indicate that 1,132 Blacks were held in slavery when the British assumed control. Farther south slavery was an integral part of American society. The American independence movement's professed support for liberty and freedom did not include their own Black slaves. The Revolution kept alive the institution of slavery in the face of a rising tide of British opposition to its continuance.

Britain exploited this hypocrisy as early as 1775 by inviting slaves to join the British side against the American rebels. Throughout the Revolutionary War they promised freedom for those who did. American victory, however, ensured slavery's maintenance until Lincoln's proclamation ending slavery and the resulting Civil War in the 1860s. It provided a foundation for American policies of segregation lasting into the second half of the 20th century.

It was a legacy that might have been prevented with a British victory. Instead British North America after the American Revolutionary War consisted of largely English-speaking Atlantic Canada, French-speaking Quebec and great expanses of wilderness and scattered settlements of First Nations in today's western Canada and Ontario (then known as Upper Canada). The British moved quickly to subdivide and settle the latter territory.

Only in these places could their authority ensure that evolving and progressive British ideas on race received practical definition. In 1793 the Upper Canada Abolition Act, supported by Lieutenant-Governor Simcoe, freed slaves who came into the province and further said that a child born of a slave mother would be freed at the age of 25.

Britain's enlightened policies were clouded, however, by political exigencies. On the one hand 3,500 free Blacks who had fought on Britain's side in that American war settled in Nova Scotia and New Brunswick and a further 2,000 slaves fled to Canadian freedom behind British lines during the War of 1812, but on the other hand, white British Loyalists, fleeing north in the late 18th century, brought 2,000 Black slaves with them.

This contradictory picture of free Blacks alongside those in slavery is a kind of metaphor for the Black experience in Canada—neither as absolute in its imposition of second-class status as in the United States nor as benign and accommodating as white Canadians have believed.

The British Parliament legally abolished slavery in all British North American colonies in 1834 and for fugitive Black slaves this was like a welcome mat. British motives were at least partially self-serving. Free

Blacks were particularly eager conscripts in defending their new-found freedom against any American incursion. They supported the various militia units defending British North America against unofficial American attacks during the Upper and Lower Canada Rebellions of 1837–38.

Canada was a land of promise. An "Underground Railroad" brought upwards of 40,000 fugitive slaves into Canada by the time of the American Civil War. This Underground Railroad was actually a series of "safe" houses, supported by "conductors" located along the way, throughout the United States, which protected fleeing slaves. Canadian courts, for their part, refused to extradite those who crossed the border unless they had committed crimes in the United States. Many Blacks settled in the Windsor and Chatham areas in southwestern Ontario while some opted for the larger centres of Toronto, Hamilton and the region around St. Catharines, while others went further north into the Queen's Bush and even into the Owen Sound area.

They founded their own communities. Josiah Henson established the Dawn community near Dresden in southwestern Ontario in 1834, four years after his flight from slavery in the United States. It is generally assumed that he was the model for Harriet Beecher Stowe's leading character in her book *Uncle Tom's Cabin*. Black immigrants formed societies, cautiously participated in the larger community life and started their own newspapers. One escapee, Mary Ann Shadd, became the first female editor of a newspaper in North America in 1853. Other famous escapees included Harriet Tubman who returned to the United States at least 20 times to assist 300 other slaves fleeing to Canada.

By the middle of the 19th century, however, the British gradually transferred more administration to local control as the threat of American invasion receded. Canadian settlers were more equivocal than their British masters in matters of race. Like their neighbours in the northern United States, they rejected the institution of slavery but often supported separation of the races. Poorly educated in a wilderness environment, white Canadians in Ontario were like their counterparts in British Columbia who opposed Chinese and Japanese immigration. In both cases the white population claimed these minorities worked for lower wages when, in fact, it was their visible difference that offended them.

Canadians in Ontario had some degree of local control over education before Confederation. Segregation had been permitted with passage of the Common Schools Act in 1850. Toronto was an exception to this practice.

William P. Hubbard, an honour student of the Toronto Model School in the 1860s, later became the city's first Black alderman and acting mayor.

The 1860 case of John Anderson also brought the fugitive slave matter to a head. A Canadian court ruled he should be returned to the United States for having committed a murder during his escape from slavery. Behind the scenes, however, the British Governor General, Sir Edmund Walker Head, with the active support of the British Colonial Office had decided that regardless of the verdict they would not turn Anderson over to the Americans. These bewigged and often foppishly depicted British authorities had taken an extraordinarily bold stance. They would soon hand over local administration, however, as the colony achieved nationhood in 1867. From that point forward Canadians would decide the fate of their Black citizens.

Black settlement wasn't limited to Ontario. Some slaves had fled to British Columbia at the time of the Fraser River gold rush during the late 1850s and early 1860s, but the longest established Black communities were in Atlantic Canada. Unlike Ontario, where both fugitive slaves and "free" Blacks arrived in large numbers in the 30 years before the American Civil War, Nova Scotia was home to Black Loyalists from the time of the American Revolutionary War, along with rebel Maroons deported from Jamaica following their defeat in 1789 Second Maroon War which had erupted in defiance of the island colonial government. Many were deliberately placed on unproductive land, however, and gravitated in time to their own communities like Africville in Halifax.

Africville was created in the middle of the 19th century as a separate Black community. Located in the north end of the city, it grew around its churches. These not only provided an unofficial link to the white community but also assumed a crucial role in educating students abandoned by the mainstream educational system.

Its citizens helped build Halifax and were an important part of its service industry. The placement of railroad tracks, sewage disposal facilities and other unwelcome urban infrastructure contributed to Africville's decline in the 20th century. By the time of Canada's centennial in 1967, the refusal of public officials to invest in the community's maintenance ensured its decline. Residents were relocated and Africville was eventually demolished.

In the United States the American Civil War provided for the emancipation of its Black population. At first the prospects for newly freed slaves looked good. Black universities and schools were founded, state

One face of Canada—The all-Black Coloured Diamond Baseball Team of Halifax, Nova Scotia, circa 1920s. *Courtesy of Photography Collection, Public Archives of Nova Scotia.*

legislatures welcomed elected Black politicians, and constitutional rights were extended to guarantee citizenship and voting rights. The short-lived Freedmen's Bureau was part of the process of rebuilding a stable union after the war. This reconstruction period generally lasted from 1865 to the withdrawal of federal troops from the American south in 1877.

Gradually, however, a reaction set in among America's white population characterized by fraudulent race science theories depicting Black citizens as intellectually inferior. Separate public facilities in everything from schools to washrooms became common practice. New polling taxes, literacy tests and intimidation by white terrorist organizations like the Ku Klux Klan quickly reduced Blacks to second-class status. It was a policy later adopted in South Africa.

This dark period of discriminatory laws and customs known as Jim Crow, after an old minstrel song, culminated with the 1896 Plessy versus Ferguson case legalizing educational segregation as long as schools were separate but equal, a standard seldom enforced.

Canadians deplored these more overt American apartheid practices but, as their actions dating back to the 1850s showed, they often betrayed a peculiar ambivalence when it came to condemning racism in all of its forms.

Another face of Canada—the integrated line-up of a Moose Jaw, Saskatchewan, baseball team, the 1895 territorial champions.

Black Canadians were never certain as to how genuine their welcome had been. At the end of the Civil War many of them believed prospects were better in their former homeland. They began returning to the United States, a migration that continued even after the initial positive steps there were undone. From a high of around 60,000 residents at the start of the American Civil War in 1860, Canada's Black population had shrunk to fewer than 18,000 by the turn of the century.

Black Canadians were discouraged by the experiences of groups like the all-Black Victoria Pioneer Rifle Company, formed from the ranks of those invited in 1858 to Vancouver Island during the gold rush days. Though they defended Victoria from potential American incursion and supported British Columbia's eventual entry into Confederation, they were barred from public ceremonies. The British rejected their appeal for official status as an established regiment. When it became clear that the United States would not invade this part of Canada, the company disbanded.

Black communities, with a few notable exceptions, were separate from white society and became an almost invisible part of the country's history. Over the next century, there was no great influx of Blacks as there had been prior to the Civil War. The majority of those who came did so as individuals or as family members. Some were Americans fed up with that country's segregation practices; others were job-seeking emigrants from the West Indies.

There were only a few occasions when Blacks arrived as part of a larger contingent. At least 1,000 Black Oklahomans moved into the northern prairies between 1909 and 1911. Despite their small numbers, they encountered prejudice. Between 1921 and 1951 the small Black community in Alberta fell from just over 1,000 to 700 persons.

Many Alberta farmers were white Americans. In April 1911, their anti-Black sentiments were inflamed by the story of a 15-year-old Edmonton girl who accused a Black man of assault. Newspapers attacked the "Negro Menace" and the "Negro Atrocity" only to be silenced nine days later when the girl admitted she had made up the story.

In that same year Albertans sent a petition to the Prime Minister. It read, "It is a matter of common knowledge and it has been proved in the United States that Negroes and whites cannot live in proximity without the occurrence of revolting lawlessness and the development of bitter race hatred, and that the most serious question facing the United States today is the Negro problem…There is no reason to believe that we have here [in Canada] a higher order of civilization, or that the introduction of the Negro problem here would have different results."

Descendants of early African-American immigrants to Alberta around the turn of the century are found in this photograph of the all-Black Amber Valley Baseball Club in Alberta, circa 1950. *Courtesy of Glenbow Archives, NA-704-5.*

Anti-Black sentiment flourished in other parts of the prairies. In Saskatchewan there were upwards of 10,000 Ku Klux Klan members or their sympathizers by the end of the 1920s. Likewise in the more urban areas of eastern Canada, the majority white population continued to oppose Black entry into jobs and integrated neighbourhoods, claiming it would cause social turmoil as in the United States.

Within their isolated communities, Blacks had few institutional supports beyond the church. They attempted to develop a self-sufficient economic base but their communities weren't large enough to support either an independent farming lifestyle or their own businesses. Many Blacks were forced to seek manual labour in nearby cities or join the growing ranks of porters working for the various railroads.

During the First World War, an unwritten policy of the Canadian armed forces discouraged Black participation because it would, supposedly, drive away white volunteers. Despite this propaganda, the all-Black Number Two Construction Battalion was formed with a majority of recruits from Nova Scotia. During the war, a Black Canadian soldier Jeremiah Jones distinguished himself by capturing a German machine gun post.

American Blacks, meanwhile, were beginning to experience a cultural flowering of their own. The Harlem Renaissance's geographic impact in the 1920s went far beyond New York City. It was sparked by literary, musical and artistic expression. The jazz and blues recordings of American Blacks of this age are part of a legacy reputed to be the only true American musical innovation. A renewed sense of Black pride found expression in organizations like Marcus Garvey's Universal Negro Improvement Association.

In Canada, where numbers were small and spread over great distances, a cultural and organizational renaissance of this scope was almost impossible. Following an example from the American labour movement however, a Canadian union of sleeping car porters marked an important step forward for Black community organization. Their leaders included Winnipeg's Piercy Haynes (whose non-railway interests included boxing and jazz) and his wife Zena, a jazz singer. Religion was also important, particularly organized churches like Winnipeg's Pilgrim Baptist Church and the African Baptist United Church in Nova Scotia.

The struggle for racial equality, however, would be fought largely in the United States. It had begun with the campaign to end slavery culminating in the American Civil War. It continued through the imposed burdens of Jim Crow legislation and it included proposals by some leaders for a return to Africa.

By the time of the Second World War, the American Civil Rights Movement, through the National Association for the Advancement of Colored Peoples (NAACP), focused on removing legislated restrictions and creating opportunities for full participation in American economic life. Canadians were often bemused spectators.

Blacks for instance had to fight for the opportunity to join Canada's armed forces in the Second World War. Ironically during this period Black American writers like Richard Wright found Canada a refuge from the unpleasant features of segregated American life. But in Nova Scotia, conditions differed little from those south of the border. Theatres in Cape Breton for instance maintained separate seating and as late as the 1950s restaurants in Dresden, Ontario, refused to serve Black patrons.

Organizations like the CBC provided Black American entertainers with a televised forum from which they were often shut out in the United States. At the same time Canadian Blacks remained outside the country's mainstream. However, the Canadian Negro Women's Association, founded in 1951, laid the foundation for future Black events like Toronto's annual Caribana celebration and Black History Month. They protested policing practices and media improprieties and offered scholarships for promising students.

Canada's small Black population lacked political clout but that soon changed. Great Britain began closing its doors on further emigration from the West Indies in the 1950s and encouraged other Commonwealth countries to open their doors. There was a clamour for Canada to loosen its restrictions.

Black activists also worked with members of other minorities, such as the Jewish community, to entrench human rights protection in Canadian law. By 1960 Canada had passed a new Bill of Rights rejecting discrimination based on race, colour, religion, gender and national origin.

The rising Civil Rights Movement in the United States was a powerful model for Canadian reformers. At the same time events in the British Commonwealth spurred further action. Canadians were appalled by the treatment of Blacks in South Africa, but their own immigration policy was cause for similar shame. The existing 1923 statute explicitly favoured white British applicants. In 1962 Canada adopted an immigration policy with greater regard for skill, merit and occupational needs, though often this continued to favour white Europeans.

The integrated line-up of Patterson Collegiate (Windsor) basketball team which won
the All-Ontario basketball title in the early 1940s. *Left to right:* Fred Thomas, Jack
Shuttleworth, Charlie Wells, Lyle Browning, Clarence Britten and coach Eddie Dawson. *Courtesy of Tony Techko.*

The first significant Black entry into Canada since the pre-Civil War
period began at this time. The arrival of upwards of 10,000 West Indian
female domestic workers in the 1950s eventually led to a campaign for
family reunification. Supporting legislation was passed in 1967. A more
confident Black community began to assert its political identity. Explicit
restrictions and segregationist practises were eliminated. The last legal
vestiges of Black separation, such as segregated schools, were wiped from
the books in Ontario and Nova Scotia. Black Canadians had become
proactive citizens initiating campaigns for equal justice. They created cultural events to celebrate their heritage even though subtle and systemic
racial discrimination remained.

The country gradually became a more diversified place. West Indian
immigration reached nearly 160,000 in the seventies and 115,000 in the
eighties. Caribbean immigration to Canada between 1967 and 1990
accounted for nearly ten per cent of the country's three and a half million new arrivals. This immigration peaked in the mid-seventies with
nearly 28,000 coming in 1974. Numbers declined in the eighties match-
ing similar reductions from other countries. Jamaicans accounted for

nearly 36 per cent of Caribbean immigration followed by Guyana at 21 per cent, French-speaking immigrants from Haiti at 17.4 per cent, and 13.6 per cent from Trinidad and Tobago. Sixty-six per cent of these immigrants went to Ontario followed by 26 per cent to Quebec.

There were expanded vehicles for Black entry into mainstream Canadian society. Emery Barnes was an Olympic high jumper and professional football player before becoming a long-serving member of the British Columbia legislature in the company of another prominent Canadian Black, Rosemary Brown. Abdi Mohamoud, a former member of Somalia's national basketball team, came to Canada as a refugee from civil war and helped establish the Somali Canadian Sports and Arts Centre in Toronto.

Others entered the public arena through community channels. Barbados-born Anne Cools became the first Black appointed to the Canadian Senate in 1984. Nova Scotia-born Dr. Carrie Best earned the Order of Canada for her community activism and writing accomplishments. Lincoln Alexander became the first Black cabinet minister in Canada and achieved one of the highest ceremonial posts in the country with his appointment as Ontario's first Black Lieutenant-Governor in 1985.

It may be pointless anymore to talk about a separate and united Black community, as it once was when it was generally ostracized within isolated rural and inner city enclaves. It has changed, through immigration from all over the world; disagreements among people of colour as to their identity within this description; the integration of Black citizens into the various class, income and employment categories defining the wider Canadian society; and even the problematic description of what it means to be Black, racially or culturally.

The latter has created a need for a new interpretative direction. It may be one founded on examining a rising generation described as "ethnically ambiguous" and a social context in which cultural symbols from music to clothes and language cross what were once accepted boundaries. Hence Bill Clinton was, ironically, described by some as the first "Black" President not because of his race but for his cultural references and interests.

As Lincoln Alexander has pointed out however, skin colour still makes it impossible for those broadly seen as Blacks to completely disappear into the great Canadian mosaic available to other hyphenated Canadians. The distinction of race and its particular history in Canada renders it a category, which still has meaning. There is a public tendency to assume that a level playing field exists but even successful members of the Black community often lack the kind of economic resources achieved by the white mainstream community over several generations. Blacks have had to remain somewhat wary of the larger white Canadian society. Nevertheless they have had enough confidence in their identity as members of this wider society to participate in its mainstream customs.

One of the most important of these has been sport.

2

THE SPORTING SCENE

S PORT, AS AN ELEMENT OF HISTORY, provides a lens for examining and interpreting the wider experience of Black people in Canada. It reveals life stories, which have often been ignored or bypassed. It is part of a larger North American account about an often parallel sporting culture alongside the mainstream white one. This aspect of the story has been progressively uncovered over the past 30 years, particularly in reference to Black baseball history. The Canadian experience, however, can never be submerged within a larger American context. The different historical influences, the mixture of English and French culture and the attempts to define a separate path from Americans ensures that each element of Canadian history will reveal distinct pieces of a national identity.

In a world without racial bias this study would have meaning only as a piece of one community's self-definition and evolution. Perhaps, as a result, there are few sporting histories of communities defined by ethnicity or race in Canada. Communities defined by their ethnicity have vibrant and extensive stories but their sports experiences are usually fashioned within a larger public arena. Ethnic leagues and teams have played within their own community as an extension of local community esprit de corps and not out of necessity.

Playing in mainstream leagues or broad-based competition signals for any distinct group its integration into the larger society. For groups like First Nations, Chinese, Japanese and Blacks, however, this path to integration has been more problematic. It was convenient to bar professionals from lacrosse in the 1880s as a way of effectively banning paid Aboriginal players. Many of them grew moustaches and passed themselves off as whites. Following attacks on Chinese and Japanese workers in Vancouver in 1907, the latter community adopted the novel solution of forming Japanese-Canadian hockey and baseball teams to play against white mainstream teams.

Blacks, however, faced additional challenges. Like Aboriginals and those from Asia, they were different in appearance. The history of their race's slavery and the continuing victimization of Blacks through legal means after emancipation created a unique situation. Their treatment, itself an affront to American notions of equality and liberty for all, became a kind of excuse for even more severe restrictions. White Americans demonized Blacks in grotesque racial caricatures and in daily encounters as a way of repudiating their basic humanity.

Many Canadians accepted the American belief that the races were not equal but throughout their history they often refused to introduce the practice of sporting apartheid, as in the United States. In this, as many other features of Canadian life, the reality is more nuanced and ambiguous than that available in any simple explanation.

After a brief period of tentative integration following the Civil War, Blacks in the United States were banned from open participation in most sports and could play games only amongst themselves. There were limited exceptions in sports like boxing and bicycling, and in Olympic Games participation, but even here the limited numbers indicate that athletes like Jack Johnson and Jesse Owens were exceptions to the general practice. Sports segregation continued well into the post-Second World War period. It was gradually removed through acts like Jackie Robinson's integration into organized baseball in 1946 and the eventual introduction of Blacks in the basketball and football line-ups of American colleges in the south by the 1970s. Even today there are private golf clubs that retain exclusionary policies.

Integration, however, has been a cruel double bind. The world of sports has often shortchanged American Blacks from pursuing more realistic careers. Even the successful athlete suffers. Unlike their white athletic counterparts, applauded for the well-roundedness of their intellectual and sporting pursuits, Black sporting accomplishment has often been seen as proof that members of their race had a genetic advantage in sports.

The above are largely American examples. Over the years Canadians smugly asserted their own country's more tolerant culture in race relations but, as this story of Black participation in sports demonstrates, the record is far more troubling. Canada's record in matters of race has been a disturbing mixture of occasional good intentions and ugly practices.

The story of Black athletic participation in Canada has nevertheless been a record of remarkable accomplishment in one of the few fields (the arts being the other) in which some integrated accomplishment was possible. The key word is "some" and this story is often full of heart-breaking acts of exclusion.

Canada's sporting culture is not the same as that in the United States; commercial sports in Canada have had a less successful heritage. Athletes have often had to balance their sporting accomplishment with employment in other fields. Black athletes in Canada never had the luxury of assuming that a sports career could be an occupation in itself. If they intended to make it one, they often had to move to the United States. By their accomplishments in other fields, however, African-Canadian athletes disproved the racist conclusion that they were somehow only suited to sports.

Even in its own right, however, sport is not a field of physical excellence separated from mental challenge. It is above all else a field of culture. It is as important to self-definition and expression as any branch of artistic, industrial or business life.

The Black athletic experience has been shaped by its history as a separate identity whether because of real segregation or, as in Canada, because the African-Canadian community was so small until the last 40 years. This chapter has now largely ended though there is continuing fascination with the limited number of Black hockey players in the National Hockey League. This is at best, however, a small item of curiosity.

However, an examination of Black sports participation remains a current issue in at least two ways. One of these is the problematic field of racial genetic exploration, which reduces the dynamic of public life to a lifeless debate on predetermined genetic capabilities of racial groups. In sports, as in every field, one's original talent, if that could be measured (a dubious proposition at best), only takes one so far. It is the sheer willpower, determination and dedication of the athlete that matters.

Rather than looking at genetic profiles based on absolute categories of racial definition (recognizing that 90 per cent of all Black Americans have some white ancestry), more can be gained by looking at social context. The significant involvement and success in sports by American Black athletes owes much to its being a field largely open to advancement and employment based on demonstrated ability.

The second and more pertinent area of current study is immigration. Public discussion on the meaning, necessity and challenges of integrating

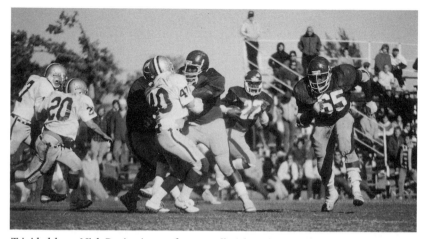

Trinidad-born Nick Benjamin was first overall pick in the Canadian Football League's 1985 draft of Canadian players. Here, Benjamin (number 65) is shown in the pulling guard position as a member of Montreal's Concordia University team where he won All-Canadian honours.

new residents into the life of the country remain with us today. Often the customs, religion, lifestyle and appearance of newcomers are different from those of the majority population.

For much of Canada's first hundred years no group, with the possible exception of the Chinese and Japanese, was more subject to these discussions as its Black population. In some ways that conversation continues though sports provides a partially liberating resolution by bringing communities together.

This examination will uncover forgotten stories of tribulation and triumph; examples of the marvellous legacy of human diversity; the profound and often neglected strengths and contributions of immigrants; and the experiences of a community of people defined by race.

As a distinct and at times almost invisible minority in a country that most chose to come to, the experience of African Canadians is markedly different from that of African Americans. Canadian Blacks sought out and participated in most sports choosing hockey in some cases, despite its cost and nearly all-white makeup, because it was the essence of a Canadian identity they wished to celebrate.

The Black sporting experience in Canada has five distinct characteristics. The first are those athletes with deep roots in the country. They share a common 19th century immigrant heritage with new European arrivals and Loyalists fleeing from the United States. They include Ferguson

Jenkins, Herb Carnegie and Fred Thomas, the sons of American and West Indian descended parents. Jenkins as well as Sam Richardson descended from slaves who had escaped to southwestern Ontario through the Underground Railroad. Boxer George Dixon grew up in Africville, the most famous Canadian Black settlement and the home of Loyalist Blacks and Jamaican Maroons. Reuben Mayes's family dated back to the immigration of Oklahoma land seekers around the turn of the century. Among baseball player Jimmy Claxton's ancestors in British Columbia are freedom-seeking American Blacks, French Canadians, Aboriginals and Scottish immigrants.

A second group are those immigrants who arrived throughout the 1970s and '80s in the wake of changes in Canada's immigration policies. Recent gold medallists including Donovan Bailey, Mark McKoy and Lennox Lewis have a West Indian background and in Lewis's case a British one as well. Outstanding female athletes like Molly Killingbeck are also West Indian immigrants.

A third are those African Americans who have influenced Canadian sports for over a hundred years. They usually returned to the United States when

Action shot of the Toronto Raptors in their second season. *Courtesy of Seneca College.*

Perdita Felicien competing for the University of Illinois. She followed her 2003 world championship title by winning the Women's 60-metre Hurdles Final at the 2004 World Indoors Athletics Championships in Budapest. *Courtesy of the University of Illinois Sports Information.*

their sports employment ended. In 1946, baseball provided Canadians, particularly the French-speaking population of Montreal, with an opportunity to accord a lone champion, Jackie Robinson, the kind of life-affirming support that helped change the world. The Toronto Blue Jays won the World Series in 1992 and 1993 led by Manager Cito Gaston and their homerun hero Joe Carter, both later inducted into Canada's Baseball Hall of Fame despite their American citizenship. A Canadian invented basketball but its greatest practitioners have been Americans. Black American general managers, Stu Jackson and Isiah Thomas, were in charge of the Vancouver Grizzlies and Toronto Raptors when they entered the National Basketball Association in 1995. The Grizzlies later left Vancouver but Toronto's star player was the Black American, Vince Carter. Another American immigrant, Mike "Pinball" Clemons of the Toronto Argonauts, became the face of the team as first its premier player, later its coach and as a permanent Canadian resident.

A fourth category now encompasses the entire world. Ethiopian and Somali soccer teams have their own leagues in larger Canadian centres. Daniel Igali, an immigrant from Nigeria, went on to win gold in wrestling at the 2000 Olympics for Canada, while a National Hockey League star, Jarome Iginla of the Calgary Flames, is the son of a Nigerian father. In the process, the meaning of what it is to be Black is being transformed as people of colour include immigrants from Sri Lanka, the Indian subcontinent and Arabic countries. The Canadian national cricket team at the 2003 World Cup was a picture of the new Canada.

Each of the above has been a stage in the evolution of Black participation in sports in Canada as skin colour and immigration background have diminishing significance. The selection of Perdita Felicien of Pickering,

Ontario, as the country's female athlete of the year in 2003 recognized her gold medal triumph in the 100 metre hurdles at that year's world athletics championships in Paris. Hers was perhaps a final stage, as it was essentially a mainstream Canadian story without reference to racial identity. Included in this fifth and final stage are African-Canadian hockey players who no longer raise eyebrows of surprise when they step on the ice. At the same time, young Blacks can form their own teams like the BigUp volleyball team, not because they have to but because they are friends and that's what friends do.

It would be naïve, however, to suggest that the distinct story of the Black athlete in Canada has ended. Racial taunts are still heard in hockey rinks, successful Black athletes in expensive cars are stopped for no apparent reason and Blacks continue to be shut out of opportunities in coaching and ownership. Skin colour not only has been but continues to be a public issue.

The study of the Black athletic experience in Canada is not only a revealing portrait of the past but one more demonstration of some time honoured truths about human achievement and the necessity of the public order to provide open and fair forums for all to participate.

To the victor go the spoils if only he or she is given "A Sporting Chance."

PART TWO

3

CANADA'S EARLY YEARS

MARSHALL "MAJOR" TAYLOR'S TRIP TO OTTAWA in the summer of 1902 seemed a lost cause. All of his equipment, including his bike, had been lost. Walking among his fellow cyclists prior to the afternoon's races, however, he met a young Toronto amateur Willie Morton. Taylor was a professional rider so they would not be competing against each other.

"I've got a bit of a problem," Taylor told the young Canadian. "My bike got lost in transit but it's a lot like yours."

"Why not try mine then. If it fits, you can use it after my race," Morton volunteered. In true storybook fashion they each won their respective races.

Major Taylor was a rarity in those days, usually the lone Black athlete at a cycling event. There were only a few others. C.E. Marshall, a Black Canadian rider, competed in match races around the same time in British Columbia.

Taylor was an American, originally from Indianapolis, who later moved to Worcester, Massachusetts. Here, his professional success earned him enough money to afford a house in a better neighbourhood. Today Worcester's pride in Taylor is shown by plans for a monument in his memory, but while he was alive his fellow citizens took up a fund-raising campaign to buy his house and encourage him to leave town.

A few years before his Ottawa adventure, Major Taylor had arrived at the World Championships in Montreal in 1899 as the favourite in the one-mile professional event. He'd recently set that distance's world record. European promoters were already inviting him to compete across the ocean. He was featured in their premier cycling publications.

Taylor's major rivals in the championship race were the Frenchman, Courbe d'Outrelon, and the renowned Butler Brothers, Tom and Nat, who along with another brother, Frank, were among the most feared

Marshall "Major" Taylor, a pioneering Black American cyclist,
found success and support in Canada at the turn of the century.

competitors in North America. They ensured that the championship field had some of the world's most accomplished cyclists.

"Fast and furious they came around the last turn," said the *Montreal Gazette*. "Within sight of the white line, the coloured rider crouched lower than ever over his mount and made a finish that would have caused the most sensational of them all to turn green with envy."

Taylor was ecstatic. "I'll never forget the thunderous applause that greeted me and the thrill when the band struck up the Star Spangled Banner. I felt more American at that moment than I had ever felt in America," he said.

The irony of the last comment is obvious. It took a Canadian crowd to illuminate Taylor's nationality and it was in that same city, 47 years later, where the integration of modern baseball would commence with Brooklyn's signing of Jackie Robinson to play for the minor league Montreal Royals.

Nor did the Canadian connection end there.

The Butler brothers provided Taylor with his greatest challenges. Andrew Ritchie's biography about Major Taylor (1988) portrays them generously, particularly the youngest brother, Tom. He describes Tom Butler as a Boston cyclist but the family was from Nova Scotia. While they may have been occasionally ruthless in working together to deny

Above, Tom Butler's display of polite and gentlemanly behaviour to the Black American cyclist
Major Taylor has been credited with helping maintain that sport's integrated character at the turn of
the century. *Right*, Nat Butler (c. 1846–1943) of
Nova Scotia's renowned bicycle racing family
who did much to support open competition in
one of the few integrated sports of the day. *Both
photographs courtesy of the Sports Heritage Centre
of Nova Scotia.*

Taylor victory, they were generally fair-minded and accepted his right to
compete in this mainstream competition. Had they objected to his presence, as white American athletes were doing at the same time in other
sports, Taylor probably would have been barred.

Ritchie describes Tom Butler's behaviour in the 1899 season as, "Polite
and gentlemanly compared with the racism of many of Taylor's 1898
opponents. The 1899 races were marked by much greater fairness and
recognition of his [Taylor's] right to compete." Ritchie calls the Butler
brothers, liberal east coast athletes, but like the spectators at the world
championships that year and like Willie Morton a few years later, they
shared a Canadian identity.

Major Taylor's Canadian success confirmed his status as one of the greatest and earliest Black sports champions in an integrated sport. He later toured
Europe and Australia drawing the same sensational reviews earned in

Canada. He returned to America in 1904 on his way to the world's championships in Europe. In San Francisco, however, he was refused entry at restaurants and hotels. Strangers walked up to him on the street and racially abused him. His white travelling companion and good friend, the Australian racer Don Walker, rather disgustedly said to Taylor, "So this is the America about which you have been boasting in Australia?" Taylor had no response.

Canadians might think that Major Taylor's treatment by their countrymen reflected a national virtue superior to that of Americans. The full story however is not so comforting.

THE OTHER SIDE

There are few records of Black sports participation in the pre-Civil War era but this was generally true as well of white working-class Canadians who did not have the financial means or status to compete in many sporting pastimes. Nevertheless at the time of the Rebellion of 1837, Sir Francis Bond Head had described "Several waggons full of the Black population in Canada, a most powerful, athletic set of men, who of their own accord, and at their expense, had come over to the frontier briefly to beg, in the name of their race, that I would accord them the honour of forming the forlorn hope in the anticipated attack on Navy Island…."

This athleticism was no doubt a response to the kinds of manual labour available to recent Black settlers, but there are other references in pre-Confederation accounts of sporting connections. A local history of Bowmanville, east of Toronto, claims that the town's barber in the 1840s "was a coloured man named Smith. He was tall, straight and muscular, something of a pugilist, and up to all kinds of circus performances. He was here, off an on till well up in the sixties." In 1866, the *Toronto Daily Leader* newspaper condescendingly described a sleighing party involving the local Black population by noting, "…a large number of darkies were rejoicing…The ebonies were got up in great style…this most comical portion of the great human family."

But it was by the water that the first significant Black sporting opportunities emerged. So much of the economic life of new communities like Toronto depended on lakes, rivers and oceans as sources of food, power or transportation. Water taxis plied the lakeshore, schooners delivered goods, fish were caught and recreation was available.

Eli Playter's diary of life in early Toronto (then known as York) provides a small portrait of what life may have been like. On July 1, 1802, he writes, "...walk'd down on the bank met Mr. Dean & stop'd some laughfing at a little black boy in a small skiff working to get ashore in a very awkward manner & some one waiting for the Boat on shore swearing at him & frittened him out of half his witts..."

The first organized rowing competitions in Canada date back at least to 1813 in Newfoundland and the 1830s in Halifax, before arriving in Toronto by 1839. The first major competition occurred in 1848. "On those two historic days," said rowing historian Robert Hunter in 1933, "the waters of Toronto Bay fairly boiled in the wake of lumbering fours-with-keel, pairs, doubles and singles." Physical supremacy and prizes varying from £7.10 to silver sculls provided motivation for those competing in what were derisively referred to as barges. Among the early stars was Richard Tinning whose wharf was at the foot of York Street. There were no distinctions between amateur and professional. Everyone competed for money and races were often interrupted by emergency calls to save nearby sailors in distress.

ROBERT BERRY: CONFEDERATION-ERA ROWER

For working-class citizens, a rowing competition was an extension of their daily work. In the first month after the birth of the Dominion of Canada on July 1, 1867, members of the Toronto Rowing Club, the premier such organization in the country, passed a resolution "Precluding any coloured man to enter in any but the fisherman's race at the upcoming regatta." The club's president, Angus Morrison, was both a Member of Parliament and a future Toronto mayor. Their actions were directed against a man many knew and had competed against. The "coloured" man was Robert Berry, a fisherman by trade who worked for the Ward family, after whom a Toronto island was named.

A letter writer identified only as "JUSTICE" commented in the August 9, 1867, *Globe*, "Your correspondent would like to enquire...why such an order has passed in a Canadian club, where justice and freedom is claimed for all men. If the coloured man is so made inferior to all other classes of men, why should our generous Club admit one of the humblest of the people in the fisherman's race, and allow him at a former regatta to take some of the principle prizes. And if such a frivolous distinction has been forced on the coloured citizens simply on account of the colour, it should meet with the strongest disapproval by all logical men."

The *Globe* agreed with the letter writer and said, "The Regatta Club has acted unjustly, illiberally, and illogically. If coloured men are not fit to run all the races they are not fit for the fisherman's race. This is the first instance within our memory of a stigma being attached in Canada to the colour of a man's skin in an open and public manner. No injustice of that sort would be tolerated in England. It is an importation of one of the least excusable Yankee prejudices."

Another writer of August 13, 1867, and identified simply as "A Voice From the Bush" in the County of Simcoe (and possibly a Black resident for whom the "bush" often described lands such as the Queen's Bush in Wellington County which were part of the Crown reserves and therefore not open to titled ownership) wrote, "It was with feelings of astonishment and indignation, that I learned by your paper of yesterday, that the Toronto Regatta Club had prohibited coloured people from competing in their races. I am a loyal man, and endeavour to instill loyalty in others. But loyalty, Sir, implies not simply devotion to our Queen, but attachment to the constitution, to the laws, and to the force of moral feeling which prevails in our country. Now, Sir, I contend that the constitution, the monarch, the laws, and the people of Britain frown upon this miserable distinction of colour—a distinction which is nothing less than an insult to our Creator.

"I lament that in the capital of the Province of Canada, and in the midst of all the light which extended education and science throws on our days, such an outrage on the fair fame of England should have been perpetrated. I look upon this war of colour as a vile Republican prejudice, imported from our neighbours...

"Let me remind them that one of the greatest men of whom England could ever boast, Dr. Samuel Johnson, appointed his servant Francis Barber, formerly a slave in Jamaica, to be his residuary legatee, a position which no British nobleman would have objected to hold...

"God grant we may have no repetition of doings so unseemly and anti-British."

Robert Berry was one of the first significant Black athletes in Canada in an era in which records are sketchy. He was a friend of the Tinning boys, the Ward family and later Ned Hanlan, the greatest Canadian athlete of the 19th century. One year before Confederation, Berry combined with J. Durnan, son of the lighthouse keeper, and W. Montgomery to row their boat *Silver Arrow* to victory and a prize of $30 at the annual regatta of the Toronto Rowing Club.

This club, formed in 1856 with clubhouse and rowing quarters at Tinning's Wharf, was captained by E.G. O'Brien. Over time separate prizes were provided to the gentlemen amateurs of the club. Fishermen were assumed to have an unfair advantage because their occupation contributed to their prowess. Such logic was eventually used to rationalize the establishment of the amateur movement. Although elitist in character, that movement was not explicitly racist.

This lithograph, *A Sculling Match—Toronto Harbour,* circa 1870s, captures the atmosphere in which Bob Berry competed, The rower may, perhaps, even be somewhere in the scene.

Robert Berry competed against the leading rowers of his day including Richard Tinning's son, Richard, who once cajoled Berry into practising starts all morning before a race in Lachine, Quebec, and then easily beat him in the afternoon. On another occasion John Scholes, who ran the Athlete Hotel on Yonge Street, outraced Berry over a three-mile course near the northern elevator on Toronto Bay. According to Hunter, "Mr. Scholes at the start of the race proceeded to induce Mr. Berry into an argument which reached such heights of passion that Berry was left mumbling to himself." Berry practised with the great Ned Hanlan himself though their age difference made a challenge unlikely by the time Hanlan was world champion.

In 1867 Berry was permitted to compete only in the fisherman's race. He lost. His crew "that has distinguished itself in previous years, was poorly handled, and under proper management should have taken the race," the *Globe* reported.

A WATERFRONT HERO

In 1872 Henry O'Brien, son of the Toronto Rowing Club's first captain, established the Argonaut Rowing Club. It became the new elite organization dedicated to making rowing an amateur sport, one that excluded professional fishermen like Berry.

The next generation of rowers like Ned Hanlan found supporters among Toronto's gambling fraternity. There would be no new "Bob Berry" because the international rowing realm in which Hanlan now moved was virtually all white.

There was at least one moment of honour left for Berry. On December 7, 1868, a heavy gale and snowstorm wrecked the schooner *Jane Ann Marsh* near the Toronto Island. Stripping to their underwear and setting out in a small skiff while the storm still raged, Berry and William Ward struggled to reach the floundering ship. Three times their own boat capsized and the careening skiff gashed Berry's head.

Ward later said, "We were seven hours at the work. When we would come ashore with a couple of them, and the men on the beach would get our boat ready for the next trip, we would run up and down in our bare feet in snow half way up to our knees to restore our circulation. We had to strip to our underclothes to have any chance fighting our way out from the undertow when the boat capsized."

Both men were awarded the Royal Humane Society's silver medal.

Many Blacks in Canada had begun returning to the United States at the outbreak of the American Civil War in 1861. Public incidents such as that involving Berry in 1867 did little to stem this choice.

A rowing contemporary of Bob Berry, the world champion Ned Hanlan in competition on Toronto Bay, May 15, 1878. *Courtesy of the Toronto Reference Library, T 13375.*

4

LOOKING OUTSIDE CANADA FOR OPPORTUNITY

Canada's Black population, confined to low-paying menial jobs in cities and often living on poor quality land in the country, faced wrenching choices of either loyalty to their new country or economic promise in the United States. Those who were athletically gifted pursued their sport outside of Canada.

THE EARLY DAYS OF BOXING

No sport before World War I offered more opportunities for integrated competition than boxing and even it was far from perfect. Ironically few other sports went to such absurd lengths to racialize potential contests. The search for "a great white hope" in boxing remains today a satiric reflection of what was once a serious proposition.

Organized boxing, or milling as it was often known, goes back to the 1700s in England. Among the serious challengers in the early years of the 19th century were two former American slaves Bill Richmond and Tom Molineaux. They both fought the English champion Tom Cribb. Matches in those days were brutal bare-knuckle affairs lasting hours until one boxer surrendered.

The spirit of those early battles crossed the ocean along with some of the first settlers in Upper Canada. Robert Gourlay's description of early problems in Ontario in 1822 included a condemnation of the vulgar sport of pugilism. Edward Talbot, another visitor during the same period, decried the general and detestable practise of boxing in the province. Through the century laws were passed prohibiting public boxing exhibitions. This sport had its roots in working-class culture, however, and laws were almost powerless against such a popular contest.

CANADA'S BOXING LEGENDS

Three of the best early Canadian boxers were born in the 19th century in Atlantic Canada—George Godfrey in 1853 in Prince Edward Island and George Dixon (1870) and Sam Langford (1886) in Nova Scotia.

George Godfrey went to sea at a young age and didn't begin boxing in Boston until he was 26. Though somewhat small at five-foot-ten, he had a long reach and deadly punch which he used to maximum effect in winning the Colored Heavyweight Championship of America in 1882. John L. Sullivan, the first officially recognized heavyweight champion of the world, once ducked a pre-arranged fight with Godfrey as the Canadian was warming up. Sullivan refused to cross the colour line.

GEORGE DIXON

George Dixon was born in Halifax's Africville, on July 29, 1870. He worked as a photographer's apprentice. When he was 16, the small-time boxers who came to the studio for publicity shots impressed him. He followed them back to the gym. He was only five-foot-three and weighed just over 100 pounds and the other fighters called him "Little Chocolate."

"Young Johnson" was the first to fall to his fists and quickly Dixon became the dominant boxer in the smoky clubs of the region. Not surprisingly he soon moved to Boston, a city then known for its racial tolerance because of its role in the anti-slavery movement. Here he met white promoter Tom O'Rourke who became not only his manager but also his future brother-in-law.

Dixon had a charmed career claiming the 105-pound paperweight title. There were only a few derogatory comments about his race perhaps because not many people paid much attention to boxing's lowest levels. Dixon soon bulked up to the 112-pound bantamweight level.

The rules of boxing were gradually reformed to restrict the number of rounds, not, however, before Dixon and a New Yorker, Cal McCarthy, fought a 70-round draw at Boston's Washington Hall. The fight lasted almost five hours. In deference to modern methods they wore two-ounce gloves, which had recently been introduced because too many boxers were breaking their fingers.

George Dixon, the photographer's apprentice from the
Africville community in Nova Scotia, became a boxing
world champion. *Courtesy of Canada's Sports Hall of Fame.*

George Dixon's next stop was England. World boxing titles were generally bestowed only after both American and British champions had
been defeated.

Important changes were occurring in the British attitude towards Blacks.
The country had become the premier colonial power and its Empire encom-
passed territory in Africa, India and the far east. Darwinian principles were
manipulated to rationalize the subjugation of other people. Now African
Blacks, Chinese and those from the Indian sub-continent were considered
racially inferior and dependent on the largesse of the imperial power.

Tom O'Rourke however was a persuasive salesman and after several weeks of negotiations got Dixon a shot at the acknowledged world bantamweight champion, Nunc Wallace. The Canadian was an immediate sensation, displaying his scientific style by shadow boxing in front of a mirror and using a punching bag. In June 1890 he knocked the Englishman out in the 18th round.

Any American doubts were dispelled soon after when Dixon won a 40-round decision over Johnny Murphy in Rhode Island. With little fanfare, Dixon, the Canadian, had become the first Black man to ever win a world boxing title.

He then moved up to the featherweight level. He knocked out both the American and British champion and confirmed his title with a victory over Fred Johnson at New York's Coney Island in 1892. Later that year, however, his life was endangered while defending his title against the amateur titleholder Jack Skelly in a three-day Carnival of Champions at the Olympia Club in New Orleans. Ringside spectators burned Dixon's legs and others lashed out at him with billy clubs. The local Ku Klux Klan threatened to kill him. He was spirited out of town. Fights between Blacks and whites were soon banned in many places.

Dixon fought all over the United States in title and exhibition bouts. For a time he was considered the most famous Black man in the world. He lost the title in 1897 but regained it a year later, becoming the first titleholder to do so.

On January 17, 1899, two Black fighters fought for the first time in a title match as Dixon knocked out a South African challenger "Young Pluto" (Joe Brown) in New York City. Constant touring, alcohol and drug abuse, and public displeasure at his marriage to a white woman combined to wear down the gifted fighter. On January 9, 1900, he lost his title forever to Terry McGovern. He continued to fight in matches lasting 20 rounds and moved to England for two years. Dixon died nine years after losing the title. He was penniless and perhaps punch drunk from over 800 bouts.

Eventually he was honoured as a member of Canada's Sports Hall of Fame. The City of Halifax, which he had left to become one of boxing's greatest pioneers, named a recreation centre after him. His gravesite in Boston reads simply, "Here lies George Dixon, the gamest pugilist who ever lived."

Sam Langford from Weymouth, Nova Scotia, was a great heavyweight.
He was never given a chance to fight for the world title. *Courtesy of
Canada's Sports Hall of Fame.*

SAM LANGFORD

Sam Langford was born in 1886 on a dirt-poor farm in Weymouth, Nova
Scotia. It was a land of deliberately low quality soil. It had been given to
previous Black immigrants who thought their loyalty to the Crown would
be better rewarded. His father worked as a part-time sailor, part-time
logger and occasional farmer. Sam, one of seven children, was beaten
regularly and, by the time he was 14 years of age, he fled to Boston to
work as a bartender's assistant.

Poverty and punishment prepared Sam Langford for the fight game.
He was introduced to a retired pharmacist, Joe Woodman, who told the
young Nova Scotian, "You got no business fightin' amateurs. I know where
you can get some money." That's all he wanted to hear. Langford turned
pro and Woodman became his manager.

Over a career spanning more than 600 bouts around the world, Langford, nicknamed the "Boston Tar Baby," occasionally fought the leading
contenders of his era but more often fruitlessly pursued a title bout in
the higher weight divisions. At five-foot-six, or thereabouts, and fighting around 170 pounds, he was outsized by most of his heavyweight rivals.

He chose this level not only because it offered the greatest opportunity for money and acclaim but because his extraordinary reach of 84 inches compensated somewhat for his size.

The higher levels of the sport attracted the greatest public attention on the race issue. Nat Fleischer, editor of *Ring Magazine*, once rated Langford the seventh best heavyweight of all time, but the Canadian never got a championship fight. Langford beat Joe Gans, the light heavyweight champ, in a non-title bout, but the loser refused him a rematch for the real thing. Promoters for middleweight champ Stanley Ketchel promised him a title shot in return for a pre-arranged no-decision exhibition. Langford acquiesced, but his hopes were dashed when shortly after their fight an irate husband killed the philandering white champion.

For years Langford fruitlessly pursued Jack Johnson for a heavyweight title shot. Johnson was an American Black and the first man of his race to win the title. Johnson reasoned that there would be little public interest in a fight between two Black boxers. In any case, they'd met two years before and the American had soundly beaten the novice boxer. Johnson was also at odds with the National Sporting Club (NSC) in England.

Before his title fight with Tommy Burns in Australia in 1908, he had promised the club that his first match after that fight would be against Langford at the NSC. This extraordinary opportunity to match two of the best fighters in the world, despite the fact both were Black, spoke highly of that Club's sportsmanship. In return for that promise the NSC paid Johnson's fare to Australia, but he was subsequently accused of squandering that money on "High speed automobiles, white women, diamond necklaces, chicken and champagne." When he asked for more money, the NSC balked.

He got to Australia, however, and won the title from the white Canadian, Tommy Burns. White commentators forever after blamed the Canadian for giving the Black fighter this opportunity. Burns, born Noah Brusso, was from Hanover, Ontario, and made his first mark as an exceptional lacrosse player competing against Native Canadians, despite the objections of others. Author Dan McCaffery says Burns was unwilling to accept American practices barring Blacks from competing fairly in sporting contests. Burns said he would duck no man. Though it's claimed that the Canadian didn't accept the equality of the races, it's also said he didn't dislike Blacks. According to Joe Louis in a 1978 interview, Burns was one of the few whites who not only wouldn't draw a colour line, but he'd go drinking with his Black opponents after a fight.

Sam Langford knocks out an unnamed opponent in 1911. *Courtesy of Canada's Sports Hall of Fame.*

Having beaten Burns, Johnson reneged on his promise to the NSC thus denying Langford a title shot. The champion returned to England in 1911, after fleeing the United States following his conviction under the Mann Act for entering into an inter-racial relationship. He was refused entry at the NSC and an October fight with the British champion was cancelled due to pressure from non-conformists of the Free Church Council. These non-conformists pressed for, and got, a ban on any Black fighter challenging for a British championship. The NSC fell in line with others in supporting this ban on Black contenders. They were still miffed at Johnson and launched a stinging and racially abusive attack on him.

In the decade prior to the First World War, race was boxing's dominant issue. Before 1908 Johnson and other Blacks had fought for a Negro heavyweight championship. His win over Burns made that redundant. Former champ Jim Jeffries, defeated convincingly by Johnson in 1910, said, "I want to see the championship come back to the white race where it belongs."

The first modern boxing champion, John L. Sullivan, said, "Let them fight among themselves and the whites among themselves. The minute a white man matches with a Negro he invites and deserves a licking." In response to Johnson's title victory there was even a brief flirtation with a "white heavyweight championship." The concept ended tragically in 1913 in Calgary where the supposed great white hope, an American, Luther McCarty, lost the title to a Canadian from Chatham, Arthur Pelkey. McCarty dropped dead in the ring without suffering a blow. An autopsy revealed he had probably broken his neck in a horse-riding accident a few days before.

In that same year the most distressing edict in Canadian sport was handed down when the boxing committee of the Amateur Athletic Union of Canada announced that "No coloured boxer will be allowed to compete in the Canadian championships…" because, "competition of whites and coloured men is not working out to the increased growth of the sport." Black athletes, it seems, were winning most of the fights and the white boxing establishment was not amused.

Langford fought only once in his native Canada and by then he was long past his peak. He easily won his Toronto bout in 1921 against a young Black Canadian, Peter Jackson from Windsor. Toronto newspapers described the large turnout of the city's Black population for the fight and ridiculed, in racially demeaning terms, the banquet held afterwards in Langford's honour.

Langford was eventually recognized in Canada and in Weymouth, where some family members still lived, but his remaining years were spent in the United States. He sank into poverty and was supported in his later years by the sporting fraternity. He was hired to sit in bars and regale listeners with tales of boxing's old days.

Boxing's most noted scribe of the 1950s, A.J. Liebling, said Langford once told him his secret, "Whatever that other man wants to do, don't let him do it."

LARRY GAINS

Britain's colour bar showed how far the country had drifted from its progressive views on race in the mid-19th century. The ban lasted longer than even baseball's racial prohibition in the United States. Its effect was particularly harsh on another Black Canadian boxing export.

Larry Gains left Toronto in 1923 where he'd been born on Sumach Street in the heart of Cabbagetown in 1900. He claimed at the time to be embarrassed at still living at home. Another fighter, Soldier Jones, encouraged him, "You know, Larry, I think your style of boxing would go down very well in England. Over there they like a man with a good left hand."

Gains took a cattle boat to England and fought his way to an outdoor show at the Leicester Tigers Athletic Ground for the British Empire title in June 1931. Before 35,000 people he beat the reigning British champion, Phil Scott, in two rounds, winning the crown. Gains also out-boxed the Black American heavyweight, Obie Walker, at the same grounds in July 1935 in a contest billed as the "Coloured Heavyweight Championship of the World."

Gains is not well known in North America because he did so much of his fighting in Europe. He eventually settled in Cologne, Germany, where he died in 1983. Among his noteworthy conquests, however, were those over two future heavyweight champions, the German, Max Schmeling in 1925, and the Italian, Primo Carnera in 1932. He fought until the Second World War but never got a British title fight, owing to the continuing ban on Black fighters. A world title bout also eluded him.

It's unlikely he would have had better fortune in North America. Another Black Toronto fighter, Little Arthur King, fought out of Philadelphia in the 1940s. The notorious gangster "Blinky" Palermo managed him. It was an era of shady dealings and fixed fights and, though King beat the finest lightweights of the time, he also never got a title shot.

Larry Gains of Toronto, British Empire Heavyweight champion in the 1930s. *Courtesy of
Canada's Sports Hall of Fame.*

In the midst of war the British Boxing Board of Control's ban on Black boxers was discussed in the House of Commons on July 31, 1941. The Secretary of State, Herbert Morrison, after consultation with boxing authorities concluded, "Spectacular fights between opponents of different colour" should not be encouraged and therefore coloured boxers should not be allowed to fight for British titles.

Despite the presence of Black citizens in the British army fighting against Nazi Germany, the boxing ban was not lifted until September 1947, more than two years after the war had ended.

5

BLACK BASEBALL'S EARLY DAYS IN CANADA

ASEBALL'S LONG HISTORY in North America makes it a particularly useful case study of the way in which Canadians and
Americans dealt with the issue of race. The game developed at the
same time in both countries though Americans played a leading role in
the development of its rules and organized structure. The ways in which
Canadians responded to these initiatives tells us a lot about the country.

Informal bat and ball games were played in Ontario's white community in the 1830s at the same time as in the United States. Organized teams
appeared by the mid-1850s again alongside American developments.
Newly arriving Blacks from the United States may have first seen the game
in Canada around this time. In any case, by 1869 an all-Black team, the
Goodwills of London, Ontario, played the all-Black Rialtos of Detroit.

Formal separation of Blacks and whites in baseball was not as yet
accepted practice but its future character was reflected in opponents faced
by the Guelph Maple Leafs. In 1874, they played the Ku Klux Klan club
of Oneida, New York, at a tournament in Watertown, New York, and a
year later hosted the all-Black barnstorming team, the St. Louis Black
Sox. By virtue of being locked out of organized baseball, Black baseball
teams were virtually all of a barnstorming character except for the short-
lived years when they could join all-Black leagues.

White Canadians were unsure of how to react to the integration of
Black players in their games and by default usually let Americans make
those choices for them. American players on the London Tecumsehs 1878
International Association team objected to the presence of Black players
on rival mixed teams. In 1881, members of the Guelph Maple Leafs

refused to play alongside an American Black professional, Bud Fowler. He eventually played several games for an integrated Canadian team in nearby Petrolia, Ontario.

There are many examples of Canadians in other sports welcoming the opportunity to play against Black athletes, but the white Canadian baseball establishment was either ambivalent or actively opposed. In 1887, James "Tip" O'Neill from Woodstock, Ontario, and the greatest Canadian ballplayer of the 19th century, came down firmly on the side of segregation. He was the ringleader of his St. Louis Browns' teammates in petitioning club owner Chris Von Der Ahe, against playing an exhibition game with the all-Black Cuban Giants.

It read, "We the undersigned, do not agree to play against Negroes tomorrow. We will cheerfully play against white people at any time, and think by refusing to play, we are only doing what is right, taking everything into consideration, and the shape the team is in at present."

Though it's unclear, white ballplayers may have been concerned about the threat posed to their jobs by talented Black players. At the other end of the income scale, poor and recent white immigrants to the United States saw Blacks, moving into northern cities, as competitors for low-paying jobs.

SEGREGATION TAKES HOLD

By the 1880s gifted Black ballplayers were challenging whites for baseball employment. The generally sympathetic treatment of Blacks during British rule and the underground flight of slaves to Canada before the American Civil War had given way in 20 years to simple-minded racist descriptions of the crudest character.

In 1887, the *Hamilton Spectator* described Newark's George Stovey and Moses Walker as a "coon battery" and suggested that the "coloured population have a monopoly of the calcimine business." The paper said of Stovey, "He is everlasting smoking cigars when he is off duty and looks as if he had just succeeded in colouring himself a trifle." To its credit, the *Spectator* later apologized to the city's Black population and blamed a careless editor for the story.

Throughout baseball history the Irish, Germans, Italians and, more recently, those from the Dominican Republic all suffered ridicule and stereotypical analysis. Only Blacks, however, were banned from the game's mainstream. In 1884, a few Black players had been able to participate in at least one major league, the American Association. As the decade progressed others played in a variety of minor leagues.

As Jim Crow legislation reduced Blacks to segregated second-class status in the United States throughout the 1880s, organized baseball also took a harder line on minority players. Teams were initially discouraged from hiring Blacks. Eventually, common practice became the unwritten law.

Toronto and Hamilton were members of baseball's International League. Teams in this premier minor league had been early leaders in signing Black players. In late 1887, as the spirit of exclusion swept through organized baseball, the league formally decreed that no club "Should promulgate contracts with colored players." Not only were Canadians, as members of the league, complicit in these actions but also Torontonians taunted Buffalo's Black player Frank Grant with cries of "Kill the nigger."

The only role remaining for Blacks in the International League was the demeaning one of mascot for its segregated white teams. The Toronto team appeared in Rochester wearing maroon caps and shirts, and breeches with gold belts. They attributed their victory to a "Very small fat coloured boy who they acquired in Syracuse as their mascot."

Several lower ranked minor leagues continued to hire Blacks until the end of the century. Alex Ross, a Black Canadian, played in the Northern Michigan and Michigan State League from 1887 to 1889. He was one of over 70 Blacks playing organized minor league baseball in this period. One of his teammates, in 1889, was Bud Fowler. With a few notable exceptions, however, Blacks were totally excluded from organized baseball by the start of the 20th century.

The actions of Canadian teams in the International League were not an unfortunate exception. The Western Canada League's reputation was tarnished in 1910 when it banished one of its players because of his apparent racial background. That season had gotten off to a good start in Saskatoon with the 30 strong 22nd Saskatchewan Lighthorse Regiment striking up the music for a 5:30 start. In Regina, Dick Brookins from St. Louis had been signed to play third base and the *Regina Leader* reported on April 12 that the "Hard hitting Indian...will hold down the awkward corner." Two weeks later he had three hits, two stolen bases and two exceptional fielding plays in an exhibition game at the team's spring training site in Lacrosse, Wisconsin.

Brookins started the season but both Medicine Hat and Calgary claimed, "He has Negro blood in his veins." Regina responded by confirming his Native status. In the pecking order of baseball apartheid,

Aboriginal background was slightly less contentious than Black.

The matter was referred to baseball's National Commission, which oversaw organized baseball. On May 26 the *Leader* reported that the editor of the *Sporting News* said, following enquiries to the National Commission, that no dispute could be found to Brookins' eligibility. Furthermore "Brookins' people are well known residents of St. Louis and live in a neighbourhood exclusively for whites and are classed as white."

Nevertheless league teams persisted in their complaints. In early June rumours circulated that Lethbridge's manager Chesty Cox was about to be fired, but not before Regina had induced Cox to trade Lethbridge's first baseman to Regina. Benton Hatch, a Lethbridge official, was furious at losing this player and retaliated by questioning Regina's continuing employment of Dick Brookins. He said he would ensure "the nigger did not play anymore." Brookins heard the comment and threatened to fight Hatch if he didn't apologize. The next day Medicine Hat asked for a ruling and league President Eckstrom banished Brookins, despite the absence of a ruling from the National Commission.

Brookins disappeared into the anonymous life of the itinerant ballplayer. A Regina paper declared, "Neither Brookins or the club has received anything like a square deal, nor the faintest suspicion of British justice being in evidence the way the case has been handled."

Nor did this occur only at the professional level. So thoroughly did Canadian baseball defer to American control in the 1920s that amateur authorities in Ontario wrote to the Commissioner of Baseball, Kenesaw Mountain Landis, to enquire as to whether a Black youth could play in a local Ontario championship. Organized baseball by virtue of its ban on Black major league players was shamefully ill-equipped to pass judgement over a matter in which, in any case, it had no jurisdiction.

LOOKING FOR WORK AND PLAY

If they wanted to continue playing, Black athletes had to pursue what amounted to a parallel existence. For baseball-playing Black Canadians this situation forced them to go south of the border for employment either with one of the many Black barnstorming teams or in the poorly organized Negro leagues.

Hipple "Hippo" Galloway born in Dunnville, Ontario, played a variety of sports on mixed teams as a youth. In 1899, he was a member of a Woodstock hockey team and that same year he played 20 games with Woodstock's Canadian League baseball team. In St. Thomas he appeared nervous and the crowd taunted him.

His release was hastened either by a .150 batting average or the comments of rival players such as Hamilton's McCann who refused to play against him. Despite the urging of many Woodstock players to stay, he left the town and the country to play baseball for the Cuban Giants.

Ollie Johnson of Oakville, Ontario, had played senior baseball in his hometown in 1916. In search of better competition he joined a Buffalo based all-Black barnstorming team, the Cuban Giants. After

Hipple Galloway, a two-way athlete in baseball and hockey, had to leave Canada to find sporting employment.

his baseball days he returned to Oakville where he became a respected elder statesman of Oakville recreation before his death in 1977. He was awarded lifetime membership in the Ontario Baseball Association.

John Joseph Evans was born in 1911, the descendant of American slaves who had escaped to Canada. His father sold railroad bolts to the Canadian Pacific Railway at the turn of the century. J.J. started playing baseball seriously in southwestern Ontario in the 1920s. At 16, he was playing for a local senior team, Walker House.

Barnstorming American Black teams visiting Detroit would often make the easy trip into southwestern Ontario for exhibition games against Windsor's all-Black Mic Macs. "If Windsor players were good enough," Evans says, "they would often leave with the team they'd just played against and begin their baseball career."

Evans went to Detroit when he was 18 years of age, playing most positions with, among others, the Detroit All-Stars, the Detroit Giants and other Negro League calibre teams in Chicago and Philadelphia. "Fifty dollars a game, that's what I used to get. It ain't nothing of what you'd get today for the calibre of ball that I played. I should have been in Willie Mays' place, pulling his salary."

'EE-NUT
'ERIES
'916
CLAXTON
OAKS

Jimmy Claxton from Wellington, British Columbia was the first Black player to appear on a trading card, the Zee-Nut Series, with the 1916 Oakland Oaks of the Pacific Coast League.
Courtesy of William Weiss.

At Toronto's Varsity Stadium in the 1930s, he ran against and beat another Black Canadian athlete, Sam Richardson, reputed to be the fastest man in Canada. He played baseball with Satchel Paige, Josh Gibson and Buck O'Neil. His Canadian rivals included the all-rounder Fred Thomas, as well as Fergie Jenkins's father.

Evans went to Europe with the Canadian Army in the Second World War and afterwards played fastball with the Joe Louis Punchers. An industrial accident in 1948 ended his baseball career. In later years he was active in local minor baseball in Ajax, Ontario.

One Black Canadian had an unusual first. Jimmy Claxton born in 1892 in Wellington, British Columbia, was of mixed Irish, English, Black, French and First Nations background. His family left Canada when he was a baby and settled in Tacoma, Washington. He eventually played a few games with the Oakland Oaks of the Pacific Coast League becoming unwittingly the first known person of Black ancestry to play in organized baseball in the 20th century. He was also the first to be portrayed on a baseball card, released by Zee-Nut in 1916.

Some Black Canadian ballplayers, however, were able to stay home. Baseball had tremendous growth in the late 19th century in Atlantic Canada. A number of all-Black teams were formed including the Halifax-based Eurekas who lost only one match in the 1890s. Other teams were the Truro Victorians, a Dartmouth squad, and the Independent Stars and North Ends of Halifax. The Celestials of Fredericton, New Brunswick, barnstormed with the Victorias of Halifax in 1891. By the end of the century there was an annual maritime championship for Black clubs.

In Saint John, New Brunswick, an all-Black team, the South End Royals, played in the city's mainstream South End League. Their star player was pitcher Fred Diggs and they won the championship every year in the early twenties. In 1922 they also won the intermediate championship of Saint John.

In Alberta, Black Oklahomans had settled in Amber Valley, originally known as Pine Creek, near Edmonton. Seventy-five of the original 95 Black homesteaders remained through the first war and later the Depression, despite hardships ranging from insect invasion to premature frost. They cleared enough land to receive homestead patents and, beginning in 1915, the community held a picnic drawing people from as far away as 50 miles. Baseball games were its central focus.

Members of First Nations, along with Métis (the descendants of Indian and French-Canadian parents), were Amber Valley's closest neighbours. Inter-marriage was not uncommon. In return for teaching them such northern survival skills as woodcraft and tanning, Blacks taught the Indians how to play baseball. The Black community in Amber Valley survived until the Second World War and their team toured northern Alberta. After 1945 it began to decline as young people sought better jobs in Edmonton or Calgary.

Many Black Canadian ballplayers went to the United States for work, but, reversing that flow, American Black barnstorming teams came to Canada looking for new markets. Tours by these teams were common between the two world wars. They relished the opportunity to travel without restriction on the Canadian Pacific Railway. It was a precarious existence, however, and faded once the better Black players began entering the major leagues after 1946.

In the same period, one of the best Canadian Black teams was the Chatham, Ontario, Colored All-Stars. They had formed in 1932 to make a few dollars barnstorming throughout Ontario. The players, in their late teens and early twenties, couldn't find work in their own town because of their skin colour and the effects of the Depression.

Despite some questionable umpiring decisions, they won the Intermediate "B" provincial title in 1934 against the Penetang Shipbuilders led by a future major league pitcher Phil Marchildon. The two teams had split the first two games. In the deciding game, Chatham had taken the lead in the top of the 11th, but in the bottom of the inning, with one out, the game was suddenly stopped on account of darkness. A lengthy dispute followed in which it got increasingly darker, making the original decision moot.

The game was played over in its entirety on October 23 in Guelph with Chatham easily winning 13-7. The *Globe* reported, "The difference between the two teams today lay in the fact that 'Big Flatfoot' Chase, the Chatham pitcher, was able to come back inside 24 hours while Marchildon, the young Penetang hurler, was troubled with a sore arm." Don Tabron recalled that a hotel in Penetang had slammed its doors on them but one in nearby Midland welcomed them.

A final recognition was accorded the team in 2002 when the Toronto Blue Jays wore replicas of the All-Stars' old double knits in a game with the Boston Red Sox as part of a commemoration for the old Negro Leagues. Chatham, of course, never played in those leagues, having found a way to play in an imperfect but still somewhat integrated world of senior baseball in Ontario in the 1930s.

JACKIE ROBINSON

"I owe more to Canadians than they'll ever know. In my baseball career they were the first to make me feel my natural self."

Jackie Robinson's moving words described the magical summer of 1946. He faced many verbal attacks in the United States when he became the first Black player in organized baseball in the modern era. Fans of the hometown Montreal Royals of the International League, however, greeted him hospitably and affectionately.

Ironically, the year before, Richard Wright, an esteemed Black American writer of the middle decades of the 20th century, had also found greater acceptance in Canada than in his native United States. He wanted to go to France at the end of the Second World War but because of travel restrictions spent two months in Quebec living anonymously on the Ile d'Orléans. Historian Robin Winks says, "He savoured the financial independence that the mounting sales of *Black Boy* were giving him and sought out 'a way of living with the earth' rather than, as in New York, 'against the earth'. "

Quebec was seen as an island of calm refuge on a continent torn by racial division. French Canadians saw themselves as a people apart. Perhaps in the struggle of the Black community they sensed a common

Jackie Robinson, as a member of the 1946 Montreal Royals. *Courtesy of the National Baseball Library, Cooperstown, New York.*

despair. Pierre Vallières acknowledged this position in his autobiographical work *Nègres blancs d'Amérique* (1968), which was translated in 1971 into the more pointed English title, *White Niggers of America.*

This theme had been publicly broached as far back as the election of 1948. Quebec nationalist André Laurendeau called the provincial premier, Maurice Duplessis, a "Negro king," for his resemblance to a tribal ruler in one of Britain's African colonies. By extension French Canadians must have been his "Negro" subjects. For Laurendeau, the British counterparts in Quebec were the Anglo owners of industry who funded Duplessis' election campaigns in return for his quiet acquiescence in

Left, John Wright, signed by Branch Rickey to join Jackie
Robinson, *right,* with the Montreal Royals in 1946. Wright
didn't make the team and Robinson went on alone.

maintaining their low wages for the French-Canadian working class. Writing in *Le Devoir*, Laurendeau said, "They dominate the Negro king but
they allow him fantasies.... One thing never comes to their minds, and
that is to demand the Negro king conform to the high moral and political standards of the British."

These politically loaded observations, however, were founded on a dubious comparison. Quebecois had never experienced slavery, Jim Crow
legislation or explicit segregation. Nevertheless Quebec became the focal point
for one of the great moments, not only in sports, but in 20th century life.

Even as Richard Wright was celebrating the relative freedom his time
in Quebec afforded him, Branch Rickey, general manager of the Brooklyn Dodgers was scouting players in the Negro Leagues for the ostensible
purpose of starting a new all-Black league that would play in Brooklyn's
Ebbets Field when the Dodgers were on the road. Among the players that
impressed Rickey was a former Southern California football star and ex-
soldier, Jackie Robinson. Robinson was good enough to step directly into

Once a fervent opponent of baseball integration, Montreal Royals'
manager Clay Hopper, shown with player Sam Jethroe in 1949,
came to accept changing times. *Courtesy of Library and Archives
Canada, C66757.*

the Dodgers' line-up, but Rickey wanted to see how he would handle
himself in a setting out of the major league spotlight. Montreal was the
perfect location.

Rickey's decision to sign Robinson and a lesser-known Black player,
Johnny Wright, to minor league contracts created only mild interest in
Quebec where integrated competition went back at least to the mid-1930s.
In 1935, Granby's team in Quebec's Provincial League (QPL) had signed
a Black player, Alfred Wilson, away from Chappie Johnson's Colored All-
Stars. The All-Stars were virtual members of the Provincial League that
summer, playing an ongoing series of games with league members to
help keep it financially solvent.

In 1936 and 1937, the QPL included the Black Panthers, a team of Black
defectors from both the United States-based Negro League and some barnstorming teams. In July 1936 the QPL announced plans for its first all-star
game. Fans elected a team scheduled to play the Montreal Royals of baseball's International League at Delorimier Stadium, the Royals home

ground. Three Black players, Carl Logan, Ormond Sampson and Hank Chaffen, were among those selected. The game started late, at 9:15, so that fans from outside Montreal had time to get to the ballpark. Several of the southern born players with Montreal, however, refused to play against the integrated QPL team. Rather than call their bluff, organizers, after some debate, shamefully told the Black players they would not play, nor would they collect their share of the gate receipts.

Ironically, ten years later, one Montreal reporter would claim that Robinson's signing proved that the Canadian city was the most democratic place in the world. An American, Tom Meany, boldly stated, "Rickey felt he had the ideal spot in which to break in a Negro ballplayer, the Triple A farm in Montreal where there is no racial discrimination." The *Chicago Defender* editorialized, "It is ironical that America, supposedly the cradle of democracy, is forced to send the first two Negroes in baseball to Canada in order for them to be accepted."

Robinson could not be sure, however, of his teammates' support. His manager, Clay Hopper, a Mississippi native with a financial interest in the cotton industry, was against integration. One day in spring training, Hopper asked Rickey, "Do you really think a nigger's a human being?" Hopper also had a hard time with French-Canadian players on his team, once calling pitcher Jean-Pierre Roy a "French son-of-a-bitch."

Montrealers on the other hand welcomed Jackie and his wife, Rachel, graciously. Answering an advertisement to rent an apartment on Rue de Gaspé in the overwhelmingly French-speaking east end, the Robinsons nervously wondered if they'd be rejected as usually happened in white American neighbourhoods. Instead the proprietor invited them for tea, offered them the use of her kitchen and bedroom supplies, and leased the apartment without question. Rachel Robinson later said, "It left us euphoric. All the months in Canada were like that."

He probably had little contact with Montreal's predominantly poor, working-class and small Black community, who lived in the west-end neighbourhood of Saint-Henri among other similarly impoverished French Canadians, who were immortalized in Gabrielle Roy's *Bonheur d'occasion* (1945). Pianist Oscar Peterson was born here and rose to musical fame under the enforced and often harsh tutelage of his father, an accomplished amateur musician, who worked as a sleeping car porter. Railroad work and domestic service were the limited jobs available for, respectively, Black men and women in Montreal. Their small numbers contributed to an invisibility which limited more explicit discrimination beyond the workplace. When a talent like Oscar Peterson entered Montreal's mainstream, however, he encountered the same derogatory slights practised in other Canadian cities, as at least one hotel refused him entry to perform. Only the threat of bad publicity made them raise their prohibition.

Jackie Robinson appears never to have had such experiences in Montreal. In the next few months, a white sportswriter, Sam Maltin, and his wife, Belle, befriended the Robinsons. Sam described himself as a Jewish socialist. He wrote for the *Montreal Herald* and also for sympathetic American papers like the *Pittsburgh Courier*. He and Belle took the Robinsons to classical concerts of the type Rachel had enjoyed in Los Angeles. They introduced them to Herbie Trawick, whose team, the football Alouettes, made overtures to Robinson about playing for them. Jackie had been a star player at UCLA but Rickey forbade any two-sport ambitions.

Just before the start of the 1946 season, a nervous International League president, Frank Shaughnessy, warned Rickey about possible race troubles in Baltimore should Robinson appear. He asked him to reconsider his decision. Rickey chose to ignore him and Robinson debuted in Jersey City before a sold-out crowd of 25,000. He went four for five and electrified the crowd in the 5th with a bunt single, followed by a stolen base, and then went to third on an infield out. As the Jersey pitcher went into his motion, Robinson streaked for home but stopped halfway, causing the pitcher to halt his delivery. The umpire called a balk and waved Robinson home.

Afterwards enthusiastic Blacks mobbed him. It was a scene repeated in other International League cities. In Toronto, the *Globe and Mail* noted, "Robinson's appearance on the diamond last night brought out quite a few of Toronto's coloured colony."

Robinson led the league with a .349 batting average, scored a league leading 113 runs and swiped 40 bases. The Royals defeated Newark in the first round of playoffs and then eliminated Syracuse to advance to the Junior World Series title against Louisville. Fans in the southern city taunted Robinson unmercifully and, after winning the first game, the Royals fell behind two games to one.

Returning home the team was heartened by their fans' response. "We discovered," Robinson said later, "that the Canadians were up in arms over the way I had been treated. Greeting us warmly, they let us know how they felt... All through that first game [at home] they booed every

Sandy Amoros and Chico Fernandez of the Montreal Royals, 1953. The Brooklyn Dodgers continued to sign Black players while other teams hesitated. *Courtesy of Library and Archives Canada, C66866.*

time a Louisville player came out of the dugout. I didn't approve of this kind of retaliation, but I felt a jubilant sense of gratitude for the way Canadians expressed their feelings."

Nor was the fans' reaction the only uniquely Canadian touch. During a game in early October the temperature dropped below the freezing point. Despite having taken a 4-0 lead, the Kentucky team succumbed to the taunts of 15,000 fans and the weather. Louisville's pitcher walked the bases loaded in the 9th and the Royals scored two to send the game into extra innings. Jackie Robinson drove in the winning run in the bottom of the 10th.

Milder weather brought out nearly 18,000 fans for game five and, again, Robinson starred as his booming triple in the 7th put him in position to score the winning run. For good measure he bunted home Al Campanis with two out in the 8th. In game six Robinson was brilliant both in the field and on the base paths. In the 8th, the Louisville pitcher went through a routine of fake throws and real ones in an unsuccessful attempt to pick Robinson off first and then second. The crowd howled.

The Royals protected an early 2-0 lead for a series victory. Robinson was mobbed by jubilant Montrealers who cried "Il a gagné ses épaulettes." He was carried about the field in a scene so moving that Robinson's friend

Sam Maltin wrote, "It was probably the only day in history that a Black man ran from a white mob with love instead of lynching on its mind." It remains the greatest moment in Montreal baseball history.

Robinson went on to a hall of fame career with the Brooklyn Dodgers but the historic import of Robinson's role and play in 1946 lifted a minor league title into the realm of the mythic. A solitary human being and a city had confronted society's worst demons and for a brief moment triumphed over them.

Robinson's breakthrough was one of the first significant steps in the fight for equal rights following the Second World War. Canadians have rightly celebrated the important role they played in Robinson's ascent.

A NEW BASEBALL ORDER

The final stage of baseball's separate existence followed the collapse of the Negro Leagues after the integration of organized baseball. Some of that league's stars began drifting into the semi-professional leagues in Canada.

Shanty Clifford, a baseball immigrant to Canada, shown playing in the Dominican Republic. Clifford got three home runs in this game.

Jimmy Wilkes, an American baseball immigrant to Brantford, Ontario, in the 1950s. He had previously starred on one of the many Black barnstorming teams.

Luther "Shanty" Clifford, Wilmer Fields and Jimmy Wilkes played in Ontario's Inter-County Major Baseball League in the 1950s and early 1960s.

Wilkes and Clifford were two of the small number of Black American emigrants to Canada in the first half of the 20th century. Wilkes first played pro ball with the Newark Eagles in 1945. He came to Brantford in 1952 as part of a barnstorming team, the Indianapolis Clowns, for whom Hank Aaron once played.

"I went five for five. The local people liked me. I told them I was tired of riding around the country and if they were interested they should call me. They phoned over the winter and I came up in 1953. Opportunity only knocks once and if you don't take advantage it never comes again.

"I played till 1963 and when I retired they gave me a night. I was making money playing in Brantford but when the fans give you something you really appreciate it." Wilkes stayed in Brantford. He married, worked for the city and became a respected local umpire.

Clifford, his Brantford teammate, had played for the Homestead Grays and Kansas City Monarchs in the late forties. Like Wilkes, he took advantage of the opportunity to put down roots. He was the Inter-County League's batting champion in 1956.

Wilmer Fields was the best of the former Negro Leaguers who came to Canada. He had been the ace of the Homestead Grays' pitching staff starting in 1940 and led that team to the last Negro National League championship in 1948. The major leagues didn't offer enough money so he went to the Inter-County League.

He won that League's Most Valuable Player award in 1951 in his first year in Brantford. In 1952, Jack Kent Cooke paid him $14,000 to join Toronto's International League team. He returned to the Inter-County League in 1954 hitting .379 for Brantford, and then .425 for Oshawa in 1955, before returning to the United States in 1956.

6

SPORTING IMMIGRANTS AND THEIR DESCENDANTS

S TATISTICS APPEAR TO SUGGEST that people arrive in a new country as part of a larger group. In fact they usually come alone or with only their immediate family. Emigration is a lonely business and for none more so than visible minorities.

JOHN WARE

John Ware, a pioneering creator of the modern rodeo, is one such story. He was not the only Black person to make his way to Canada's west, but his story is well-documented. Born a slave on a South Carolina cotton plantation in 1845 he was freed only at the end of the Civil War, 20 years later.

Freedom for former slaves often meant a new form of indentured servitude of low wages, little legal protection and no social support system. Ware went west and worked on a Texas ranch. He was part of the Black cowboy era in the United States. He became an experienced cowhand driving herds of cattle between Texas and Montana and sometimes as far north as the foothills near Calgary, Alberta.

The area appealed to him as did the settlement enticements of the Canadian government. Local folklore suggests many other Black Americans came to Alberta in the 25-year period between 1880 and 1905. Ware worked for local cattle companies before starting his own ranch in 1890. He married and raised a family. He was a great rider but his fame was ensured when by accident he "invented" steer wrestling, one of the central features of modern-day rodeos.

Alberta cowboy and rancher, John Ware, posing with his wife and two of his children, Robert and Nettie, in front of their home. *Courtesy of Glenbow Archives, NA-263-1.*

While working in a corral beside the north fork of the Oldman River in Alberta in the spring of 1892, he reacted instinctively to a charging longhorn cow. He grabbed its horns and held on while it dragged him across the corral. Reaching his arm around the cow's head and grabbing hold of its nostrils he managed to twist the head and bring the animal down with all four legs pointing skyward.

Later that year at a local equestrian show, known popularly as a gymkhana, he demonstrated the rudiments of a new technique. It was a sensation. At the Calgary Fair the next year, a steer roping and tying contest was held. The $100 saddle prize was won, of course, by Ware who roped, threw and tied a steer in a time of 51 seconds. The sporting aspect of such shows began to replace skills demonstration and the competitive rodeo began to take shape, out of which the Calgary Stampede would emerge.

Dubbed the Negro Cowboy, Ware's legendary status was furthered by his untimely death in a horse riding accident in 1905. A mountain, a creek and a gulch were all named after him using his supposedly affectionate nickname, Nigger John. Locals claimed this nickname was not a slur and they regarded him highly. A folk song was written in his honour and his log cabin was moved to a provincial park as a semi-official shrine. Today his full name more appropriately adorns a college building in Calgary.

BOXING

Black athletes, like Ware, were tiny beacons of individual achievement. Boxing offered viable employment opportunities. Joe "Dad" Cotton, a former slave born in 1853, had fought as a heavyweight on the American west coast, as well as in Australia and England. He came to Edmonton in 1912 and opened a boxing club.

Cotton refereed locally and, though over 60, had one last fight in Drumheller. He won by a knockout. He belonged to a local Black church, organized an all-Black lodge and was a leader in Edmonton's boxing community until his death in the 1950s.

Other prominent Alberta boxers included Harvey "Flash" Bailey, Canada's flyweight champion in the 1930s; western Canadian welterweight champ Bennie Geary; and Vern Escoe, the Canadian heavyweight champ in the forties.

FOOTBALL'S NEW ARRIVALS

Football, because of its popularity in both the West and East, is a better indicator of racial attitudes. The Canadian Football League was not integrated until after the Second World War. The story starts in the east. As it had done in the early days of Confederation, rowing played an ironic role.

In the 1930s, a Black Simpson's Department Store shoe salesman named Hackley was part of Toronto's rowing culture. But issues of minority participation in either football or rowing seldom arose owing to the small size of Canada's Black population. The Toronto Argonaut Rowing and Football Club was the fulcrum for a major change.

Many rowers in the 1870s despaired at the activities of the Toronto Rowing Club. They viewed it as not much more than a social organization, good at organizing regattas and providing comfortable chairs for aging out-of-shape men to put their feet up and ruminate on the problems of the world. Some of them may, though no such record exists, have regarded that club's deliberate exclusion of Robert Berry at the 1867 Regatta as an affront to common decency.

In any case, the Argonaut Rowing Club was organized in 1872 by Henry O'Brien, son of one of the founders of the Toronto Rowing Club. A year later a football organization, bearing the rowing club's name and coached by H.T. Glazebrook, took the field to play their lone game that season (a 3-0 loss to the University of Toronto). The football club was a place for the off-season training of rowers, but by the 20th century it gradually became the best-known public image of the Argonaut Club.

In 1946, the Argonaut football club remained a nice source of revenue for the rowers who retained ownership. Led by the brilliant Canadian tandem of quarterback Joe Krol passing to receiver Royal Copeland, the Argos were coming off a Grey Cup thrashing of the Winnipeg Blue Bombers.

The Canadian Rugby Union oversaw Canadian football in those days. It permitted teams to import up to five Americans. Lew Hayman managed a new team in Montreal, the Alouettes. They brought in six players knowing only five could stay. Hayman signed an Ohio State guard named Bill Willis who asked if he could bring along a friend, Marion Motley.

Hayman agreed but there was one problem. Football south of the border, as it did in Canada, had a colour barrier. A new league, however, the All-American Conference had recently started up as a rival to the National Football League. The owner/manager of the Cleveland Browns, Paul Brown, was anxious to sign Black players like Willis and Motley. When he got the go-ahead, the Alouettes' plans were scuttled. Willis, however, felt bad about this development and recommended that Hayman sign a young, and Black, lineman, Herbie Trawick from Kentucky State.

"I was the Montreal coach, in day-to-day contact with the players when the thing started over Herb, and I don't believe there were any problems within the team or even with opponents on the field," Hayman later said.

There were problems however. The Argonauts had opted not to sign any Americans. They were further angered by Hayman's plan to play football games on Sunday because of their professed deep religious convictions. When they discovered that the Alouettes also had a Black player, they behaved in a manner hardly different from their 1867 Toronto Rowing Club ancestors.

"The first calls that came to me were about a week before the season was to begin," Hayman recalled. "And there were follow-up calls. What they said was that we just didn't have Sunday games in the league and we simply did not use Black players. I replied that I couldn't find anything in the rules against either one."

Toronto along with Ottawa threatened to boycott games with Montreal. Their stand was ironic. Jackie Robinson had just reintegrated organized baseball in the spring of 1946 with the Montreal Royals Triple A baseball team and his visit to Toronto to play the city's Maple Leafs was relatively uneventful.

Hayman had worked as coach for the Argos in the thirties. He rightly guessed that the Argonaut club management were pompous, small-minded windbags without even the courage of their pathetic convictions. "I told them to do as they liked because if they forfeited, it would be the easiest two points I'd ever picked up," Hayman said.

The stuffed shirts of the Argonauts caved in completely and the wrong their predecessors had perpetrated on a lone rower was not repeated. Herbie Trawick, the first Black player in the Canadian Football League, had a Hall of Fame career in Montreal though his team lost to the Argos that fall in the Big Four final as the Krol-to-Copeland combination won another Grey Cup.

Hayman's team finally won the Grey Cup in 1949 and the next year the Argos would hire two Black players, fullback Billy Bass and halfback Ulysses Curtis. They won another Grey Cup and followed again in 1952. Five years later a syndicate headed by *Toronto Telegram* publisher, John Bassett, bought the team from the Argonaut Rowing Club.

In 1980 the Argos hired Willie Wood, a former Green Bay Packer player, to be one of the first Black head coaches with a professional football team anywhere. Unfortunately, the Argos continued their losing ways under his leadership and he was fired the next year after the team lost its first ten games. The club would not win another Grey Cup until 1983, when they were led by a Black quarterback, Condredge Holloway, and receiver, Terry Greer.

Black American football players also helped transform western perspectives. Woody Strode, "Sugarfoot" Anderson, Rollie Myles and Johnny Bright were the most prominent of these new arrivals. Strode was a former UCLA and Los Angeles Rams catching star who helped lead the Calgary Stampeders to the 1948 Grey Cup.

His coach, Les Lear, in the easy jocularity of the dressing room claimed, "We have Chinese, Jewish and coloured cowboys on this team." Such banter must have been uncomfortable to past victims of easy racism. Much was made as well in the eastern newspapers like the *Globe and Mail* of Strode's "lazy running style and a pair of hands the size of a basket."

Miles and Bright were part of Edmonton's Grey Cup champions of the mid-fifties and, like Calgary import "Sugarfoot" Anderson, settled in Alberta. Virnetta Anderson, who followed her husband from Arkansas in 1952, became active in civic activities and in 1974 became the first Alberta Black elected to a City Council (in Calgary).

A FOOTBALL DESCENDANT

One of the best football players from western Canada had a sensational college career at Washington State University in the mid-1980s. This was followed by several good seasons with the New Orleans Saints of the National Football League before injuries ended his career.

Reuben Mayes from North Battleford, Saskatchewan, was a descendant of Joe and Mattie Mayes who, as leaders of a Black Baptist congregation in Oklahoma, brought settlers to the area northwest of Saskatoon in 1910. It was not an easy life. The land given to 19-year-old John Mayes, a relative of Joe and Mattie, was a muskeg swamp.

A graduation photo of Reuben Mayes, North Battleford Comprehensive High School, North Battleford, Saskatchewan.

Mattie's grandson, Murray, operated an automobile body shop in North Battleford and his son, Reuben, became the hero of North Battleford Comprehensive High School before tearing up the American College gridiron. In one two-week span in 1984, against the Universities of Oregon and Stanford, he rushed for 573 yards and eight touchdowns.

His American teammates were bemused by this unlikely sensation. Mayes recalled, "They were all so brash and confident like Americans are. They made fun of my accent and I felt some anti-Canadian feeling, like 'Who's this Canadian anyway? From where? And especially a Black Canadian. Some of them would call me a 'cheesehead.' That's what they call Canadians. I'd just kinda laugh and let it roll off. I'd prove myself on the field."

7

RUNNING FOR CANADA

ETWEEN THE WORLD WARS, Blacks formed an entire series of parallel leagues and associations in all manner of sports. The most famous were the barnstorming baseball teams and Negro baseball leagues. The thirties also marked the beginnings of a slow movement away from sporting apartheid in the United States as two American Blacks, Joe Louis and Jesse Owens, won, respectively, the heavyweight boxing crown and four Olympic track and field gold medals.

In sports like track and field and baseball, Black Canadians struggled for recognition within a less than tolerant society. For a few like Dr. Phil Edwards, an emigrant from British Guiana, the choices were personal. He had the confidence and means to surmount any restrictions. For most their choice of sport reflected economic limitations.

RAY LEWIS

Sprinter Ray Lewis felt that boxers were at the bottom of the sporting barrel and it was a sport to be avoided. Lewis and Sam Richardson were the first really successful Black track athletes born in Canada. They each competed in major international competitions in the thirties and won medals for their country. They were joined on the track by a gangling middle distance runner, Phil Edwards, who rose to the position of Canadian Olympic team captain.

Ray Lewis was Hamilton's pride at the 1932 Olympics in Los Angeles where he and teammates Phil Edwards, Jim Ball and Alex Wilson won a bronze in the 4 X 400 metre relay. Lewis and Edwards were among the small number of Black athletes who competed in those games. "There were only a handful of us and a newspaperman invited the four or five

Black athletes on the American team as well as Phil and I to a party. That was about it," Lewis says.

Ray Lewis was a lifetime Hamiltonian who was in his 90s when he died in 2003. He persevered against extraordinary odds. He had competed in picnics in Hamilton and won his first medal at the age of 11 at the Broadview YMCA in Toronto. At 17, he was overlooked for the 1928 Olympic team, despite beating the runner that eventually went. "It was difficult for a Black chap. One coach didn't want me on a team touring the United States because he said it wasn't safe to take a coloured kid to Philadelphia.

"There wasn't much money to compete. In fact, coming back from the Los Angeles games, myself and Lefty Gwynne (who had won a gold medal in boxing) sold our upper berth tickets."

Ray Lewis from Hamilton, Ontario, one of Canada's fastest quarter milers in the 1930s.

Lewis worked as a railway porter on the transcontinental train, about the only well-paying job available for Blacks in those days. He recalls, "We'd go from Vancouver to Chicago and deadhead home from there. There was a lot of single track and sometimes we'd stop for a few hours while repairs were underway. That's when I got in my practise jogging up and down the line. A lot of farmers must have wondered what this crazy guy was doing. Once outside Albuquerque, New Mexico, a guy called me a nigger and I kicked him in the head as the train pulled out."

Lewis eventually went to run at Marquette University in Milwaukee, but it didn't last. "There were no Black kids there. One guy tried to pass as a white but they stepped on his hand. I was offered a chance to compete in New York but was told the only job I could get was as an elevator operator. I told them no thanks, I'd sooner stay home and shine shoes on the train."

SAM RICHARDSON

Ray Lewis remembers Sam Richardson's body at the age of 15 wriggling like a snake after throwing a ball. Lewis wished he'd had that fantastic potential. It was a raw ability that caused Jesse Owens to say he would have to stop giving pointers to the Canadian or he'd soon surpass him.

As a 15-year-old schoolboy at Toronto's Central Technical High School Richardson won the long jump gold medal at the second British Empire Games in London, England, in 1934. "I was the number in those days," he recalled. "It was important for our community but for me it was just another track meet."

Members of Toronto's small Black community turned out to welcome him on his return. The Richardsons along with the Hubbards, Lightfoots, Sharps and Jacksons were among the city's oldest Black families. "My great-grandparents came up through the Underground Railway to the Chatham area and my grandfather went to Toronto. He worked in the Parliament Buildings. My father was a tradesman.

"I went to Central Tech and did everything there was to do—track, basketball, football. I played in the backfield. I just tried to keep from being hit. For track we ran indoors at school, and sometimes went over to Hart House at the University of Toronto or Maple Leaf Gardens."

Richardson was the Canadian favourite in the indoor track meets held at Maple Leaf Gardens. "One night I made the whole Gardens crowd stand up. They thought I'd won and I would have if I'd known how to throw my body into the tape. But the American, Eulace Peacock, just nipped me."

At the 1936 Berlin Olympic Games, Jesse Owens taught Richardson poise and to "sit down in position," by which he meant running with his legs out front and arms driving at the same time to pull the weight of his body along.

At the end of the Games, Owens and American runner Ralph Metcalfe said they'd find Richardson a job in the U.S. track scene. "They had a lot of pull in those days. But the States and I were no good. Canada was and remains all I know. Whenever I was away I always looked forward to seeing the Canadian shore."

In 1938, the *Toronto Telegram* reported that Richardson, despondent over his track opportunities in Canada, was thinking of moving to Detroit with his father. A year later, however, Canada was at war and track and field was no longer a priority.

DR. PHIL EDWARDS

Phil Edwards was a member of this group of Black athletes, but his life story reflected his upper-class upbringing in British Guiana.

Wearing Canada's colours in 21 events from the 1928 Olympics through to those of 1936, he was eliminated from competition only once—in 1928 in the 400 metre semi-final, after two first-place finishes in preceding heats.

He was born in Georgetown, British Guiana, in 1907. His family was among the local Black elite of what was then a British colony. Edwards' father was a magistrate and one of 18 children originally from Barbados. Of his mother less is known, but it is thought she came from Trinidad. In the 1920s, his parents despaired of the future for their 13 children in a colonial environment and, according to Phil's daughter Gwen Emery, they also disliked the country's heat. They moved to New York City.

The choice was curious. At least in British Guiana they were members of an elite. In America, Blacks were accorded second-class status both legally and socially regardless of their profession, wealth and stature. Emery says, "Their educational background in a British system had given them a different sense of themselves. They took their equality for granted and when confronted by obstacles found ways to go around them."

Left, Phil Edwards from McGill University and the Hamilton Olympic Club, shown prior to the 1930 British Empire Games in Hamilton; *right*, Phil Edwards wearing the uniform of New York University, assists in the carrying of his Canadian teammate, 1928 Olympic gold medallist Percy Williams, winner of the 100-metre dash.

They expected that their children would enrol in a local school in Westchester County. When this was challenged, they announced plans to start their own school by bussing in additional children from Harlem. The prohibition was suddenly lifted. They soon became leading members of New York's legal community, founding a respected law and real estate firm in Harlem. One daughter was the first Black female lawyer in New York State.

Phil studied and competed in track and field at New York University in 1927 but he wanted to run in the Olympics. As a British subject from a colony with no Olympic representation, he had to find another team owing its allegiance to the Crown. He opted for Canada because of its proximity. At the 1928 Amsterdam games he won a bronze as a member of Canada's 4 X 400 metre relay team. His choice of running for Canada may have initially been opportunistic, but it took on added meaning in the 1930s. During that decade he became a medical student at Montreal's McGill University. Here he had a little apartment on Loren Crescent, just east of the university. "He experienced discrimination here as well," says his daughter, "but had the grace and eloquence to overcome restrictions." In time he became the esteemed veteran and captain of Canada's Summer Olympic teams.

Phil was at his peak in the 1932 games. He reached the final in all of his events—the 800 metres, 1500 metres and the 4 X 400 metre relay and won bronze in each of them. In the 800, he set a torrid pace for which he had become famous. It earned him the nickname of "Old Rabbit." He led at the halfway point and appeared to be increasing it, but at the final turn he was caught by his countryman, Alex Wilson, and Tom Hampson from Great Britain. Those two raced together stride by stride with the Englishman barely crossing the finish line in first, though both broke the world's record.

Likewise in the 1500 metres Edwards and the American favourite, Glenn Cunningham, opened up a huge lead. On the back straight of the last lap Edwards extended the lead, but then in a pattern that now marked his running career, an Italian, Luigi Beccali, passed him in the final 100 yards. John Cornes of Great Britain beat him out at the finish line for the silver.

"Phil was a natural athlete," says Jim Worrall, one of his McGill teammates and a future International Olympic Committee executive member. "I don't know how much coaching he got. There was no one else who knew as much about middle distance running as Phil. He ran according to his own method of training and knowledge of tactics. He went out fast, got the lead, and tried to hold on.

"His legs were disproportionately long for his body and when he accelerated his body seemed to slump with his hip level going down two or three inches as he opened up his stride."

He was a hero to his fellow teammates. Duncan McNaughton, 1932 Olympic gold medallist, says, "He was one of my favourite people in life, but very quiet and soft spoken." Margaret Lord, a chaperon with the Canadian team, recalled, "He was a wonderful man." Remembering the often brutal character of race relations in those days, she says, "He was welcomed into the best homes in Hamilton."

Phil Edwards, medallist at three Olympic Games winning a total of five bronze medals, seen here on the podium of Olympic Games held in 1932 in Los Angeles. *Left to right*: 2nd Alex Wilson, Canada; 1st Tom Hampston, Great Britain; 3rd Phil Edwards.

By 1936 he was nearing his 30th birthday, but his close-knit family, including his younger sister Sarah, followed him across the ocean. On board ship his Olympic roommate was Sam Richardson. They were placed together for one reason—both were Black. In the easy racism of the day, it was implied that no other arrangement was appropriate. No two people could be more different. Phil was a cosmopolitan, mature, upper-middle class professional. Sam was still a kid, from a working class, hardscrabble neighbourhood in Toronto. Disgusted by Richardson's habit of eating crackers in bed, Edwards asked Jim Worrall if he could stay with him. "I already had a roommate however," Worrall recalled, "So Phil had no option. Needless to say he didn't spend much time in his room."

Edwards's tremendous drive was beginning to fade, but he maintained his competitive schedule once again entering the 800 and 1500 metre events and maintaining his place on the 4 X 400 relay team.

The 1500 metre event in Berlin is recognized as one of the great races of all time ("magnificent beyond description" said the official British report) with the favourites including Lovelock from New Zealand, Wooderson from Great Britain, as well as Cunningham and the three medallists from 1932.

Sydney Wooderson was injured in the heats but the final was still a classic. Edwards couldn't summon the same breakaway speed of four years before, but at one point in the second lap when Jack Lovelock found himself dangerously boxed in, a word to Phil was all that was needed for the gallant Canadian to let him through. It may have been the difference in the New Zealander's memorable victory as he ran away from Cunningham.

Phil's best shot at a gold medal was the 800 metre race and he led after a slow first lap. His chief rival, John Woodruff, caught and passed him but on the back straight Edwards went back into the lead and the two raced grimly together to the top of the home stretch. "There was a moment or two," recalls Worrall, "when all you saw was one torso and what appeared to be four legs running under it, and then Woodruff pulled away."

It was Phil's last competitive Olympics but his teammates had their opportunity to show their affection for the runner now generally acknowledged to be their leader. Though Nazi Germany was an avowed racist state, Phil had no apparent problems there. He was not so fortunate in London, England.

The team checked into a Canadian-owned hotel in London prior to their return to Canada. His teammate, Bill Puddy, said, "We were all tired having just come across the channel by boat. I was in the tub on the third floor soaking up and I heard someone running down the hall and yelling—'get on your clothes we're leaving.' There were about 50 or 60 of us out on the street with our bags and that's when I learned that the hotel hadn't allowed Phil to register because he was Black. Finally a Canadian official told us that it was sorted out, Phil was going in and so were we." Other accounts suggest they had to find another hotel.

Edwards joined Canada's armed forces in the Second World War. He was stationed in British Columbia, near the Pacific theatre where his knowledge of tropical diseases was invaluable. He once challenged, and

Canada's 1928 bronze medal 4 X 400 metre relay mile team featuring Phil Edwards and teammates Alex Wilson, Stan Glover and Jim Ball.

beat, in a race a particularly surly Canadian officer he felt was mistreating his recruits. After the war he worked with the Olympic team of British Guiana. It was one of the numerous occasions in which he supported the country of his birth. His dual citizenship had allowed him to compete for British Guiana in the 1930 and 1934 British Empire Games (winning gold in the 880 yards in 1934).

In 1936 he was the first ever recipient of the Lou Marsh Trophy recognizing Canada's premier athlete and was later inducted into New York University's Hall of Fame a year before his death in Montreal in 1971. In 1997 he finally joined Canada's Sports Hall of Fame.

While his track strategy may sometimes have been questioned, he was a man of great spirit, who remained for an entire generation of Canadian athletes an example of wonderful achievement and friendship beyond the confines of that day's racial boundaries.

8

LONELY YEARS
OF ACHIEVEMENT

B Y MID-CENTURY sports had become a major form of 20th century cultural expression. An athlete's colour was gradually disappearing as an explicit basis for discriminatory practice. Young Black Canadians had new opportunities. Their achievements were tempered, however, by whispers of betrayal when they failed.

THE JEROMES

The Jerome family is neatly suspended between the 1930s era of Edwards, Richardson and Lewis, and the later resurgence of track and field in Canada led by a talented roster of Caribbean immigrants in the 1980s. Harry and Valerie Jerome were the children of a Black railway porter. Harry Jerome was born in 1940 in Prince Albert, Saskatchewan, but the family soon moved to Winnipeg where Valerie was born. They eventually settled in Vancouver.

Harry Jerome made headlines on July 15, 1960, at the Canadian Olympic trials in Saskatoon where his time of 10.0 seconds tied the world record in the 100 metre dash. He was the first Canadian-born track athlete to set a world record. He would later tie world records in the 100 yards, win bronze at the 1964 Olympics and win gold at the 1966 Commonwealth and 1967 Pan American Games.

Jerome was outspoken in his advocacy for Canadian athletes, saying they needed more financial support, better coaching and improved medical attention. His occasionally disdainful attitude towards the press, who invaded his preparation with inane or annoying questions, earned him

Harry Jerome, at the centre of a photo finish in Toronto's Exhibition Stadium, in the 1960s. *Courtesy of Canada's Sports Hall of Fame.*

Harry Jerome, a Canadian sprinting star at the University of Oregon. *Courtesy of Canada's Sports Hall of Fame.*

few friends in the media. Writer Scott Young voiced a minority opinion, "Give us a few more Harry Jeromes," he said, "and let them snarl."

Canada's international amateur successes in those days were few. At the 1960 Rome Olympics much rested on Jerome's legs as a world record holder. When he broke down with a charley horse in the 100 metre semi-finals, Canadians were devastated. Canadian team officials and reporters blamed Jerome for his own problems. The team's trainer scolded the athlete. "I think the muscles that tightened were in his head," he said. Jerome stayed in the sport, however, and proved his critics wrong. "It seemed that in the 50s and 60s," Ontario track official Cecil Smith later wrote, "the public preferred athletes who did not play for keeps."

Harry Jerome earned under-graduate and graduate degrees in science at the University of Oregon and had a career in sports administration in British

Harry Jerome nearing the end of his running career in 1967.
Courtesy of Canada's Sports Hall of Fame.

Columbia. He died tragically young in 1982, but is remembered today through the awarding of scholarships in his name to deserving Black students attending either a college or university in Canada.

Harry's sister, Valerie, was almost ignored. Young Black females received little support from either their families or the sports establishment. Black Canadian women were members of a very small community. Their social expectations were limited to home, church and social service projects. Their achievements in these areas suggested what might have been possible had athletics been encouraged.

There were exceptions. Hockey player Willie O'Ree had several athletic sisters, and Herbie Carnegie wrote with pride about his golf-playing daughter who might have been a better player if only she'd stayed in the sport. The absence of strong Black female role models stifled their progress.

In 1959, 15-year-old Valerie Jerome set the Canadian record of 11.8 seconds in the 100 metres. She then set a long jump standard of 5.52 metres. At that year's Chicago Pan American Games she finished 4th in the 100 metres and 7th in the 60 metre event.

At the 1960 Rome Olympics, the Black American sprinter, Wilma Rudolph, won the 100 and 200 metres and was a member of the 4 X 100 metre gold medal relay team. She symbolized the emerging role of Black female athletes.

Valerie Jerome was not on her level, but in Canada she was an important role model. She was eliminated in the second round of the 100 metres with a time slower than her Canadian record. Her 4 X 100 metre relay team lost in the first round. Her presence, however, brought attention to a formerly ignored and discouraged group of women.

EARL WALLS

Earl Walls might have been heavyweight champ but, by 1955, having fought to the fifth ranked position in the world, he decided he'd had enough.

Earl Walls in his prime. In 1954 and 1955, *Ring Magazine* consistently ranked Earl Walls in the top ten behind champion Rocky Marciano. *Courtesy of Tony Techko.*

Earl Walls, *left*, examines Ontario boxing rules with Commissioner Merv MacKenzie, 1954. *Courtesy of Canada's Sports Hall of Fame.*

"I never got a kick out of beating anybody or knocking him out," Walls later said. He retired, raised his family, sold real estate and took an active civic role.

Walls's great-grandfather, John Freeman Walls, had come to Canada by way of the Underground Railroad in 1845, after he kept a promise to his dying master to look after the master's wife. He married her and they fled to Canada hoping to live where an inter-racial marriage might be tolerated. A few generations later Earl Walls left the family farm at 18. He pursued a railway porter's job in Toronto. It was often demeaning and servile work, but the pay with tips amounted to a decent, if modest, income.

There were no jobs available, however, and so Walls took up boxing. He beat Vern Escoe, the Canadian champ, and then twice defeated a leading contender, Rex Layne. In line for a title bout with Rocky Marciano, he walked away from the sport to assume a normal life.

FRED THOMAS

Fred Thomas (1923–1981) from Windsor, Ontario, was one of the Canada's greatest athletes. His achievements match the sporting diversity of Lionel

Conacher, Canada's athlete of the first half century. Except in the Windsor area, his story is largely unknown. He was a fifth generation Canadian whose roots went back to fugitive slaves from North Carolina and immigrants from Barbados. His grandmother and the great-grandmother of Fergie Jenkins were the Montgomery sisters. Jenkins would recall that their broad-cheeked faces and smooth skin were like that of many people from the islands.

Thomas was a brilliant basketball player, but men of his race were barred from the leading mainstream professional leagues. He was progressing through the lower ranks of minor league baseball and playing professional football with the Toronto Argonauts when a knee injury ended his higher aspirations. Still, he continued to excel in semi-professional baseball and

From 1945-49 while playing for Assumption College, Fred Thomas scored 2,059 points, third on the NCAA basketball list at the time. *Courtesy of Tony Techko.*

basketball and eventually coached. His high school coach, Al Newman, recalled that Thomas was a good hockey player and a multi-talented track star in the sprints, high jump and long jump.

Thomas was a natural athlete. He played a sport for the first time and within a few minutes appeared to have played it all his life. He had an agile mind, which quickly grasped the essential features of any game. In high school basketball, he delivered a perfect hook shot with either hand. Pundits nicknamed him "Flashie."

After serving with the Royal Canadian Air Force near the end of the Second World War, he entered Assumption College, the forerunner of the University of Windsor. In 1949 he led them to the Ontario senior basketball championship, scoring 47 points as his team swamped Toronto Central YMCA 90-56. The Toronto *Globe and Mail* called him, "The best Negro athlete in Canada."

During his career he scored over 2,000 points, mostly against American colleges. In 1945 his Assumption team beat the Harlem Globetrotters,

Fred Thomas and other members of the Assumption College team, 1948. *Courtesy of Tony Techko.*

repeating a conquest of the previous year, which Fred had missed. The Globetrotters were one of that era's finest teams. They ran up such imposing leads over their challengers that they resorted to comic antics to keep the game interesting for fans.

Fred Thomas's race prevented him from playing in the leading white professional leagues so he joined the Globetrotter organization. He played for the New York Renaissance, one of four Trotter teams, and later moved to the organization's western system as a member of the Kansas City Stars.

He was also the first Black player in baseball's Eastern League, debuting in Wilkes-Barre on July 4, 1948, as a member of the Cleveland Indians' organization. Thomas was the 21st Black to sign a contract with a team in organized baseball and the first Canadian.

Injuries ended his career at higher levels of sporting organization and he returned home. He excelled in Ontario's Inter-County Baseball League (hitting .383 for the Kitchener Panthers in 1951) and in Canada's national basketball championships (leading the Toronto Tri-Bells to the 1953 Canadian senior men's basketball title). His greatest disappointment was not being selected to Canada's 1952 Olympic basketball team.

Fred Thomas in action against the University of Toronto.
Courtesy of Tony Techko.

A Windsor park is named after him. The International Afro-American Sports Hall of Fame, Canada's Basketball Hall of Fame and Windsor's local Sports Hall of Fame have all honoured Thomas.

9

IMMIGRATION'S GREAT REWARDS

THE MAINSTREAM POPULATION in western countries has complained that new arrivals from around the world threaten existing customs, public safety and jobs. Those who do not immediately succeed are said to be a drain on the public purse, while, in the United States, those who are successful are accused by some of endangering the environment because they adopt the consuming lifestyle of the established population. No Catch-22 was ever better demonstrated.

In Canada, however, few groups have had such an immediate impact on the self-esteem and accomplishment of their new country as those predominantly West Indian emigrants who transformed Canada's sporting place in the world. They included the Guyanese-born and Toronto-raised Mark McKoy, winner of an Olympic gold medal in the 110 metre hurdles in 1992; Jamaican-born and Oakville-raised Donovan Bailey, the Olympic 100 metre gold medallist in 1996; and the 1996 gold medal 4 X 100 metre relay teammates, Donovan Bailey, Sudbury's Robert Esmie (born in Jamaica), Ottawa's Glenroy Gilbert (born in Trinidad), and Montreal's Bruny Surin (born in Haiti). As well Ben Johnson left Jamaica for Canada as a 14-year-old. He too would change Canadian sports.

BEN JOHNSON

Performance enhancing drugs had been used for years by East German athletes and others, but it was a Canadian athlete who was most notably implicated. The world's fastest human in the 1980s, Ben Johnson, was one of the record numbers of West Indian immigrants to Canada in the

Above, Canada's Ben Johnson began using steroids six years before his record-setting victory and subsequent loss of the gold medal in 1988. Time would demonstrate that Johnson was not the only one. *Right,* Ben Johnson in competition. *Both photographs courtesy of Canada's Sports Hall of Fame.*

1970s. Following his world record shattering gold medal triumph in the 100 metre dash at the 1988 Seoul Summer Olympics, a banned substance was detected in his urine sample. His handlers had apparently misjudged the time required for them to clear his system.

He was stripped of his gold medal and his world record and was banned from the sport. He was eventually reinstated and competed in the 1992 Games, but was later caught a second time and permanently barred.

The Canadian public was shocked. There had been rumours that Johnson and others weren't clean, but many rationalized that possibility by suspecting that all athletes, even the Americans, were guilty.

Johnson's guilt and the widespread belief that steroid use was common among the largely Black Canadian Mazda Optimists track club, caused an immediate schism in the Canadian Olympic team at Seoul. White Canadian middle distance runners were suspected of hanging a sign that read "From hero to zero in 9.79 seconds." Lynn Williams, a bronze medallist for Canada in the women's 3,000 metre event in the 1984 Olympics, accused Johnson's white coach, Charlie Francis, of disgracing the entire team. Some athletes and media emphasized Johnson's Jamaican background rather than his Canadian citizenship.

Johnson continued to live in Canada. Ultimately he was the one who suffered the most losing not only a gold medal but upwards of $15 million in sponsorship opportunities. Years later his "crime" was found to be more widespread than acknowledged at the time and that American athletes have been some of the worst offenders.

DONOVAN BAILEY AND BRUNY SURIN

Bruny Surin and Donovan Bailey later found themselves in the ironic situation of wanting to be disassociated from Ben Johnson while, at the same time, decrying what they saw as the hypocrisy of white Canadians. In 1996 they told *Sports Illustrated* magazine that, "Afterward all the stories referred to a Jamaican-born sprinter…all you heard were jokes about Ben Johnson. Proud Canadian one day. Jokes the next."

Bailey later claimed that Michael Farber had misquoted him in the same story and that he had really said Canada was *not* as blatantly racist as the United States. At the same time, however, he left little doubt he had concerns. "Will Canadians love a Black athlete? I hope so," he said.

Bailey won the 100 metre gold medal in Atlanta and then he and Surin and their two teammates scored perhaps an even more outstanding victory when they beat the Americans in the 4 X 100 metre relay event, which the Americans had never lost.

Bailey's career was self-engineered. He studied at Sheridan College, played basketball and established a marketing and investment consulting business before concluding, in the early 1990s, that he could run faster than the sprinters he occasionally watched. Under the tutelage of American coach Dan Pfaff, Bailey combined his impressive physique of long legs and well-distributed muscle mass with improved technique and brilliant understanding of short distance psychology. He became the world's fastest human, despite a neurological disorder in his left hip, which caused him to stride farther with his right leg than his left.

He earned further acclaim with a victory over American sprinter Michael Johnson in a 150 metre race at Toronto's SkyDome in 1997. American commentators had declared Johnson the world's fastest human following the 1996 Olympics, despite the fact that this honour is generally reserved for 100 metre winners.

Before the SkyDome race, which included a tight turn that should have benefited the American, Bailey demonstrated his mastery of mind games. He complained that organizers had sabotaged his planning. He threatened to pull out. He suggested he wasn't physically sound. He lamented his ability to get away quickly. In the race, however, Bailey exploded from the blocks. Johnson's American handlers later claimed that by doing so, Bailey had forced Johnson to overreact at the start and this had caused an injury. Johnson pulled up lame as Bailey accelerated away from him.

Mark McKoy was born in Guyana and later moved to Austria, but in his peak athletic years he won gold for Canada in 110 metre hurdles at the 1992 Olympic Games. *Courtesy of Canada's Sports Hall of Fame.*

Bailey lost his 100 metre title at the Athens world championships in the summer of 1997, though his relay team repeated its Olympic win. Bailey heralded his triumphs as that of a Jamaican-Canadian. He refused to cut his ties with the place of his birth and ironically drew comparison with the ill-fated Ben Johnson.

Bruny Surin ran somewhat in Bailey's shadow and never achieved the same acclaim but as well as relay gold at the 1996 Olympics, he won silver at the World Track Championships, gold at the World Indoor Championships, and gold at the Commonwealth Games.

He was born in Haiti in 1967 and came to Canada as a child in the mid-seventies. French-speaking Haitians had begun arriving in significant numbers in Montreal in the 1960s following the liberalization of immigration policies.

For many Quebecois their provincial image had been informed by notions of a "pure laine" of white immigrants from France, with roots dating back to the 17th century. This new French-speaking minority were clearly different from earlier Black immigrants whose first language had been English and who lived a quiet and separate existence in the west end. The new arrivals were often better educated and were not content with living in traditional Black neighbourhoods. As they and other French-speaking Blacks moved into formerly white districts, there were increased racial conflicts and the beginning of disruptive entanglements between the police and Black Montrealers.

Surin's native French-language proficiency, however, had allowed him to adjust to a new life in Montreal. As Black Canadians like Surin became part of the new multi-racial face of the French-speaking province, they brought pride and challenge to a new Quebec. His presence supported and reinforced the changes in that society.

THE FEMALE TRACK EXPLOSION

Immigration provided a generation of Black female athletic role models including Molly Killingbeck (born in Jamaica), Angela Bailey (born in England), Angella (Taylor) Issajenko (born in Jamaica), Charmaine Crooks (born in Jamaica), Jillian Richardson (born in Trinidad) and Marita Payne (born in Barbados).

Above, Rosella Thorne, a sprinter from Montreal, as shown in 1950. *Right*, Marjorie Bailey, *left*, from Lockeport, Nova Scotia, in the women's 100 metre semi-final at the 1976 Montreal Olympics. *Both photographs courtesy of Canada's Sports Hall of Fame.*

Left, Angela Bailey, one of the first of the new generation of new Canadian track stars. *Right,* Angella Taylor Issajenko finished in fifth place in the final of the 100 metre at the 1987 World Championships in Rome. *Both photographs courtesy of Canada's Sports Hall of Fame.*

Charmaine Crooks carried the Canadian flag at the opening ceremony of the 1996 Atlanta Summer Olympic Games. "So many have come and gone and so many things have happened to my teammates along the way. I just think how blessed I am to do what I do," said Vancouver resident Crooks, a competitor in the 800 metres.

Crooks and those teammates created many unforgettable moments over a 15-year period. She, along with Issajenko, Richardson and Killingbeck, won a stirring 4 X 400 metre relay on the final day of the 1982 Brisbane Commonwealth Games, as Angela Issajenko held off a surging Australian charge to give Canada a victory by a margin of .02 seconds. It was a victory repeated four years later at the Edinburgh Commonwealth Games.

The Edinburgh games had been boycotted by African, West Indian and Indian countries because of Great Britain's trading policies with South Africa. Canada supported the Games organizers, however, and attended with a team including many Black athletes.

Issajenko won Commonwealth gold in the 100 metres (1982) and 200 metres (1986), but her victories were later placed under suspicion after Ben Johnson's steroid scandal broke during the 1988 Olympic Games.

"Members of our team [the Mazda Optimists sprint group] had been taking anabolic steroids and other drugs for years," she later wrote.

MOLLY KILLINGBECK

Born in Jamaica in 1959, Molly Killingbeck came to Canada in 1972. By the 1980s she was one of Canada's outstanding female track performers, winning a silver medal as part of the 4 X 400 metre relay team at the 1984 Los Angeles Olympics.

She competed all over the world at the Olympics, the Pan-American Games, the Commonwealth Games, the World University Games, and the World Track and Field Championships. Following the Ben Johnson scandal and the subsequent Dubin Enquiry, however, her track and field career was put in doubt when she confessed to steroid use.

She'd been on them through 1982 and 1983 and then returned to using them in 1987 under a program administered by Charlie Francis. "Throughout it all, your entire focus is on performance—all your fund-

Above, Molly Killingbeck made the transition from high performance athlete to university assistant coach in 1989. *Right*, Molly Killingbeck in competition. She attained a coveted post as coach with Canada's Olympic track team. *Both photographs courtesy of Tony Techko.*

ing is based on performance and your very existence in the program is based on performance," she said.

She accepted Johnson's fall as a blessing in disguise. Otherwise, "Expectations would have increased, the pressures would have increased, his steroid use would have increased and who knows what might have happened."

Her coaching career was jeopardized as funding was withdrawn from implicated athletes. In 1992, however, Paul Dupré of Athletics Canada said that Killingbeck had performed "far and above the requirements of her sanction in educating youngsters about fair play." The funding ban was lifted.

"I feel a responsibility to stick around the sport," she said. "Athletes such as Ben Johnson, Desai Williams, Angella Issajenko, Tony Sharpe and myself helped build this country's track program. We also helped bring it down and now I feel obligated to be part of the rebuilding process."

Karen Clarke arrived in Canada at the age of ten from Jamaica and ran for the Calgary Spartans track club. She finished fifth for Canada in the 200 metres at the 1991 Pan Am games in Cuba. *Courtesy of Karen Clarke.*

In 1989 she became a sprint coach with the University of Windsor's track team, conducted training sessions in China in 1990, and in 1994 was named an assistant coach with Canada's Commonwealth Games' track and field team.

HEAVYWEIGHT CONTENDERS

The latest generation of Black Canadian boxers emerged from the immigration boom of recent decades. Trevor Berbick was born in Kingston, Jamaica, in 1954 and moved to Halifax after the 1976 Olympics. He defeated a fading Muhammad Ali on December 11, 1981, in a fight dubbed the "Drama in the Bahamas." In 1986 he won a 15-round decision over Pinklon Thomas and claimed the World Boxing Council title. By then

Lennox Lewis, the Canadian Olympic Gold medallist 1988. Raised in Kitchener, Ontario, but born in the United Kingdom, he returned there after the Olympics and as a professional eventually won the World Heavyweight Boxing title. *Courtesy of Canada's Sports Hall of Fame.*

he had applied for U.S. citizenship. Eight months later he lost the title when Mike Tyson knocked him out in two rounds.

Donovan (Razor) Ruddock was born in St. Catherine, Jamaica, in 1963 and moved with his family to Toronto a decade later. In 1989 he knocked out the fifth ranked heavyweight, James "Bonecrusher" Smith, and signed a contract for a world title fight with Mike Tyson in Edmonton in November 1989. It was cancelled, however, because of Tyson's lung infection. Others claimed that Iron Mike stood to gain more by fighting Buster Douglas in Japan. Ruddock later lost twice to Tyson, who by then was the former champion having been dethroned by Douglas.

Ruddock was also knocked out in the second round by Lennox Lewis in London in 1992. Lewis had been born in east London, England, to Jamaican parents in 1965, but moved with his family to Kitchener, Ontario, a decade later. He was Canadian amateur champion three times in his teens and represented Canada at the 1984 Olympics where he placed out of the medals.

In 1988, Lewis helped stem the national outpouring of recrimination over the Ben Johnson fiasco by winning gold as a super-heavyweight, beating American Riddick Bowe in two rounds. Afterwards Lennox concluded that his professional prospects were better under the British flag following a path originally pursued by Larry Gains. Lennox won the world heavyweight title displaying the colours of the Union Jack, though he remained a Canadian.

10

THE FRUITS OF STRUGGLE

T HE SMALL SIZE of the indigenous Black population and pre-conceived notions of appropriate activity for all females made it doubly difficult for Black women to make their mark in sports. There were isolated cases of excellence such as that of Valerie Jerome, but the big breakthrough did not begin until the 1970s. Basketball provided one arena outside of track and field.

SYLVIA SWEENEY

Women's basketball made its Olympic debut at the 1976 Montreal Olympics. Canada's team lost all five games. Its leading member, however, was Sylvia Sweeney. Born in Montreal in 1956 and the niece of the world-renowned pianist Oscar Peterson (himself born in Montreal in 1925), she would go on to become the most valuable player at the 1979 Women's World Basketball Championships in Seoul, South Korea. She was also the flag bearer for Canada's team at the 1979 Pan American Games in San Juan, Puerto Rico.

At the Montreal Olympics the 19-year-old Sweeney earned dubious fame for snapping a photo of Queen Elizabeth dining with Olympic athletes. Royal protocol officials immediately grabbed her camera and exposed the film. She was told that no one takes the Queen's photo when she is eating.

When the Queen visited the Canadian women's basketball team the next day, Sweeney was absent. "They ruined my film," she said. "I didn't want to meet that woman."

Sweeney and her fellow Canadians missed the 1980 Moscow Olympics because of a government boycott. In 1984, her team was favoured to win a medal because of the absence of eastern bloc countries. Led by the veteran Sweeney, they made it to the bronze medal game against China but underachieved, losing 63-57 for a disappointing record of 2-4.

She went on to an impressive career in film and television production. Her works include a 1992 documentary, *In the Key of Oscar*, about her uncle, Oscar Peterson, for which she was both a director and producer. It portrayed Peterson's rise from a "boogie woogie" teenage sensation to his international celebrity as a jazz virtuoso. However, she remained in the sports field as an administrator with Canada's 1996 Olympic team as assistant chef de mission and a director of the Toronto Raptors professional basketball team.

SUE STEWART

Sue Stewart assumed her place as a Black female role model on Canada's national basketball team. She went to high school in Mississauga and played on Canada's Junior National team in 1987. At Laurentian University she was part of two national championship teams.

On the international scene Stewart's team won a bronze medal at the 1991 World Student Games and had a fourth place finish at the 1991 Pan American games. Her career continued as part of the 1995 National team that won gold at an Olympic qualifying tournament. They finished 11th at the Atlanta Olympics.

Stewart became one of the first successful Canadian female professionals playing for BC69 Halle in Germany in 1993–94 before moving on to Switzerland.

CLYDE GRAY

Clyde Gray, one of Canada's most exciting post-war fighters, came agonizingly close to a world boxing championship on two occasions. He did much to revive interest in the sport.

Born in Nova Scotia in 1947, he won the British Commonwealth welterweight crown in 1973. He lost a close 15-round decision to world champion Jose Napoles later that year before a wildly supportive hometown crowd in Toronto's Maple Leaf Gardens. Two years later, he again lost a world title bout to Angel Espada in Puerto Rico and then in 1977 was knocked out in his final championship attempt. Gray retired in 1980

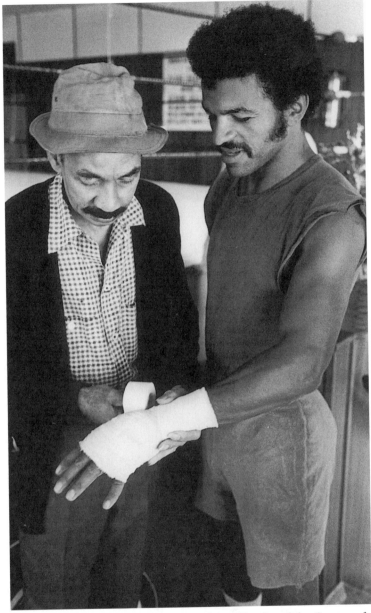

Clyde Gray, born in Windsor, Nova Scotia, preparing for a fight. *Courtesy of Canada's Sports Hall of Fame.*

and headed Ontario's Boxing Commission until 1987, thus helping usher in the next stage of Black involvement in the administrative organization of sports.

FERGUSON JENKINS—THE ONLY CANADIAN
IN BASEBALL'S HALL OF FAME

Ferguson Jenkins is one of fewer than 300 members of Baseball's Hall of Fame in Cooperstown, New York. The righthander's 284 major league wins, 594 pitching starts, career strikeout to walk ratio of 3.2:1, and seven twenty seasons in which he won 20 or more games are the stuff of record books and memories.

He was the winner of Canada's leading sports award, the Lou Marsh Trophy, in 1974; Canadian male athlete of the year on four occasions; subject of a wonderful National Film Board documentary, *King of the Hill,* produced in the early 1970s; and recipient of the Order of Canada and entitled to use the letters CM after his name.

Jenkins grew up in Chatham, Ontario, a community of 40,000 just 50 miles northeast of Detroit. Prior to the Civil War, it was a centre of anti-slavery activity and was one of the northern terminuses for the Underground Railroad bringing fugitive slaves to Canada. Ferguson Jenkins (Senior) was a third generation Canadian whose family had immigrated to Canada from Barbados. He played outfielder for several Chatham teams and, while playing, met Delores Jackson whose grandparents had come to Canada by way of the Underground Railroad. They married and their only child, Ferguson Arthur Jenkins, was born in Chatham's St. Joseph Hospital on December 13, 1943.

He claimed two traits from his mother's side. "My father says I got my size (6 foot, 5 inches) from her and my precision pitching because she was so exacting," Jenkins claimed. From his father he inherited a love for baseball and, apparently, fishing which had been the family's occupation in Barbados.

Ferguson Jenkins poses with the 1971 Cy Young Award for pitching excellence.

Ferguson Jenkins' first wife, Kathy Williams, was a descendant of Josiah

Left, Fergie Jenkins' great baseball disappointment was never pitching in a World Series. *Right*, Ferguson Jenkins as a Harlem Globetrotter. *Both photographs courtesy of Leo Kelly.*

Henson. Even with its underground heritage, however, Blacks were a minority in Chatham. Jenkins said he never experienced any racial anguish growing up in the community, though he claimed he heard racial slurs when he played outside Chatham. In his youth he was a gifted soprano who credits the poise attained in musical competition with aiding his later success on the mound. His pinpoint control dates to pitching chunks of coal from Terry's Coal and Ice Yard into the open doors of moving boxcars.

By the time Jenkins left Chatham in 1962 to begin his professional baseball career, he was already something of a local hero having played hockey for a Junior B affiliate of the Montreal Canadiens and starred in high school basketball (he later barnstormed with the Globetrotters). In baseball the limited Ontario schedule restricted his starts to seven or eight in each of three seasons of amateur ball. He later said this did not help his development, but it is possible it may have unwittingly benefited him by not placing undue stress on his arm during his formative years. He annually pitched over 300 innings throughout his major league career with little apparent harm.

Fergie debuted for the Phillies in 1965 and his first pitch put Dick Groat on his back. Pat Corrales, his catcher that day, recalled, "The next three deliveries were on the black." Jenkins later criticized such tactics. "I figure if a pitcher wants to go headhunting," he told a *Sports Illustrated* reporter, "he should play hockey instead of baseball."

Jenkins made his reputation on the strength of incredible accuracy and a slider he figured he could get in the strike zone 80 per cent of the time. He was the first pitcher to throw over 3,000 strikeouts (3192) against fewer than 1,000 bases on balls (997).

In six glorious seasons with the Chicago Cubs, between 1967 and 1972, he always won 20 or more games and the Cubs finished second and third, three times each. His greatest disappointment was never reaching the World Series.

After his major league career Jenkins played a season in Ontario's amateur Inter-County League in 1984 and in 1989 pitched in the Florida-based Senior Professional Baseball Association. He was elected to the National Baseball Hall of Fame in Cooperstown, New York, in 1991. Though he has suffered the tragic deaths of many close to him, Jenkins remains a leading advocate for baseball in Canada appearing annually at the induction ceremonies for the Canadian Baseball Hall of Fame in St. Marys, Ontario.

11

HOCKEY: THE CANADIAN SPECIFIC

C ANADIANS DEFINE THEMSELVES through a few powerful symbols—their role as peacekeepers; the length and breadth of the country, the majority of whose residents live within close proximity to the world's greatest power; and, of course, ice hockey, which may be the most important of all.

Ken Dryden and his co-writer Roy MacGregor said, "Hockey is Canada's game. It may also be Canada's national theatre. On its frozen stage, each night the stuff of life is played out: ambition, hope, pride and fear, love and friendship, the fight for honour for city, team, each other, themselves."

Poet Al Purdy called hockey "The Canadian specific." It has been a forum for much that is good and bad in Canada. Willie O'Ree, the first Black in the National Hockey League (NHL), has been depicted as the sport's Jackie Robinson, though he lacked the baseball player's superstar status. He later said, "Racial remarks were made to me during every game and after every game, and nothing was ever done about it." He applauded the NHL for refusing to tolerate disparaging remarks directed against Black hockey players during the 1997–98 season.

For Black Canadians a symbol of their integration into Canadian society is their acceptance and success playing the country's national game.

A BLACK HOCKEY HISTORY

The National Hockey League differs from other major North American team sports in its low number of Black athletes. This is largely due to the national origins of its players. Until recently they were almost overwhelmingly

Canadian. In the mid-sixties the six-team NHL had only one non-Canadian, Tommy Williams from Duluth, Minnesota, of the Boston Bruins.

Statistically the odds did not favour a large number of Black players. As late as the 1950s Canada's Black population was less than one per cent of the national total. Prior to the 1967 expansion there were just 120 NHL jobs. Nevertheless, apologists for hockey's virtual all-white makeup resorted to bizarre theories as to why Blacks couldn't play hockey. These included weak ankles, weak knees and aversion to cold arenas.

The background of NHL players has changed dramatically in the last 20 years, but this has not always improved the opportunity for Black athletes. Even though there are more jobs, candidates now come from American colleges, Russia, Sweden, the Czech Republic and other European countries. Black communities in the United States have never been hockey hotbeds. Other sports like basketball, football and baseball offered them more apparent opportunities. At the start of the 1997 season, only 22 Blacks had ever played in the NHL but in 2003, after goalie Ray Emery from Cayuga, Ontario, was called up by the Ottawa Senators, there were 15 Black players on NHL rosters, a majority of whom had learned the game in Canada.

THE EARLY PERIOD OF HOCKEY'S GROWTH

The game reached significant national fascination in the 1890s when leagues were formed, rules standardized, promoters made the leap from lacrosse to hockey and women took up the game as well as men. The first major organization, the Ontario Hockey Association was established in 1890, the Stanley Cup was first awarded in 1893 and the roots of the modern sports franchises in places like Montreal and Toronto were planted.

In the period before this, from 1860 to 1890, as young men and women experimented with a winter game played on frozen ponds and in unheated indoor rinks, the number of Blacks in Canada was plunging due to the return of many former slaves or their children to the United States. A populace of over 60,000 (nearly two per cent of the national total) prior to the American Civil War would tumble to just over 16,000 by 1911 or barely 1/5th of one per cent of the country's total. It was a community with other things on its mind than hockey, but enough examples exist to indicate an interest among Black Canadians in being part of the emerging identity of the new country.

GALLOWAY AND LIGHTFOOT

In 1899 Hipple "Hippo" Galloway, the son of Mr. and Mrs. William Galloway, described as long time residents of Alder Street in Dunnville, Ontario, played for Woodstock in the Central Ontario Hockey Association.

A Woodstock paper, under the headline "Coloured Hockey Players," reported, "Galloway is a right good sport and thoroughly game player. He withstood all kinds of punishment in Hamilton last week and fairly won his spurs. The coloured player is proverbially cool and collected so essential to hockey." His hockey record is largely unknown, though there are odd references to a two-goal night in Hamilton and a couple of excellent passes to set up goals in Paris, Ontario.

In the summer after his successful hockey season, Hipple Galloway was banished from an Ontario baseball league because an American import objected to his presence. He left Canada to barnstorm with a Black baseball team, despite a local sportswriter's plea that, "An effort should be made to keep Hipple in town. Our hockey team needs him!"

Galloway wasn't alone. Charlie Lightfoot of the Stratford team was a second Black player in the league and was recognized as one of the better players in the Central Ontario Hockey Association. Like many hockey players of the day, he soon disappeared into the myriad of available semi-professional opportunities. In 1907, hockey officials in Fort William and Port Arthur formed a professional league, the New Ontario Hockey League, with two teams from each city. Players had to be in town for 20 days before they could play. One of those was Charlie Lightfoot and his team, the Fort William Wanderers, won the league title with an 8-3 record. Lightfoot remained in the north at least through the 1909–10 season.

THE COLOURED HOCKEY LEAGUE

Atlantic Canada's large Black population provided players for what was called the Coloured Hockey League. It's unclear whether this league represented a community decision to play among themselves or if they, like players in the Negro baseball leagues in the United States, had no other choice. Nevertheless, it is an early attempt by the Black community in Canada to use sports as a means of intentionally connecting with the country's emerging self-identity.

The Coloured Hockey League of the Maritimes, formed in 1900, included teams from Africville (the Seasides), Dartmouth (the Jubilees), Halifax (the Eurekas), Truro (the Victorias) and Amherst (the Royals). It was a Nova Scotia-based league but at least one other province, Prince Edward Island, had an all-Black team featuring five members of the Mills family and two others. It played all-white teams on the Island as well as Black teams in Nova Scotia.

A majority of spectators paying 25 and 35 cents were white. Crowds often numbered 1200. They expected both good hockey and the occasional self-mockery of clowning, similar to that performed by Black barnstorming baseball teams. Fans showed their contempt if it was not forthcoming.

Exhibitions by Black hockey teams in Nova Scotia continued well into the 1920s. Their playing innovations included a rule allowing the goalie to fall to the ice to block a shot, a practice not permitted as yet in the professional game.

BUD KELLY

A league like the Nova Scotian one wasn't feasible elsewhere in Canada, but so powerful was the metaphor of hockey in the Canadian experience that Black children were determined to play the game. Their persistence throughout the 20th century attests to the game's appeal among all generations.

In the early decades of the 20th century, Frank Selke called Fred "Bud" Kelly, "The best Negro hockey player I ever saw." Kelly claimed that his first pair of skates was two whiskey flasks that he found on his father's Ingersoll farm tied to a pair of shoes. Gliding across the snow gave him his first taste of skating.

In 1916, Kelly was a member of Selke's seven-man 118th Battalion hockey team based out of London, Ontario. They played at the intermediate level of the Ontario Hockey Association (OHA). Bruce Redpath, Manager of the NHL's Toronto St. Pats (later the Maple Leafs), scouted Kelly while he was a member of Peterborough's OHA senior team. In a game against Toronto Varsity, Kelly flubbed a breakaway opportunity deliberately set up to see if he could put the puck in the net. "I was so flabbergasted by the fact that neither defenceman even laid a glove on me that I just stopped and let the puck roll off my stick," Kelly recalled. The St. Pats never called him.

Kelly did not believe race played a part in his exclusion, but we can't be certain. He had some comfort in the financial rewards provided by so-called amateur hockey. Small town entrepreneurs made payments under the table and gave players like Kelly a job, which sometimes lasted a lifetime. Kelly worked as a chauffeur for the McClary family in London for a half century.

GEORGE BARNES AND THE ST. CATHARINES ORIOLES

George Barnes, another Black player, played throughout the 1920s for Cayuga at the intermediate level of the OHA. Barnes's family were descendants of slaves who arrived in the Cayuga area by way of what was then derisively known as the "Darkey Sideroad," but later was simply Highway 56.

The St. Catharines Orioles entered in the Niagara District Hockey League. The Orioles, all of them natives of St. Catharines, were helped in their quest for uniforms by "Touch" Wood and Wally Walker of the St. Catharines Lions Club, who secured a complete outfit for the coloured stars. In the above picture, the Oriole personnel are shown, *left to right, back row*: Ben Walker (Secretary), "Chuck" Smith, Doug Nicholson, Ted Smith, "Touch" Woods (Sponsor), Alex Nicholson (Business Manager), Dick Nicholson, Amos Dorsey, Rev. J. Ivan Moore (pastor, BME Church that the Orioles represent). *Front row left to right*: George West, Ted Wilkins, Wilfred Bell, Ken Bell, Larry Dorsey, Hope Nicholson (Captain), Gordon Dorsey, and, in front, little Sylvia Moore, the Orioles mascot.

According to Dunnville historian E.G. Hastings, "In a contest in Cayuga on December 30, 1929, with Caledonia as the visiting team, Barnes was involved in an incident in which an Indian player on the Caledonia team, Wid Green, received a severed muscle in the groin and succumbed from loss of blood. I was the referee at this game and it was recorded as the first known hockey fatality in the O.H.A." Barnes also had a nephew, Sam Bright, who played for the Fort Erie Spears of the Niagara District Hockey League in the late 1940s and early 50s.

References to lone players like Barnes and Bright might suggest hockey playing was an isolated exception in the Black community. The Black population's continuing decline made any organized activity difficult to maintain. In St. Catharines they had numbered in the thousands prior to the American Civil War. The 700 Black citizens in St. Catharines at the start of the 1930s fell in population to just over 200 seven years later, as jobs disappeared for those most socially vulnerable.

It was here, however, that we have proof of the game's deep roots in Canada's Black community. In the 1930s the estrangement of Blacks and whites, at least on the sporting field, was gradually lifting. Outright separation practiced in the early decades of the century gave way to inter-racial meetings in mainstream activities.

Sometime in late 1936, H.G. (Touch) Wood, owner of Dominion-Consolidated Transport, and florist Wally Walker, of the St. Catharines Lions Club, went down to the British Methodist Episcopalian Church on Geneva Street and told members of the Black community they were prepared to sponsor a hockey club. The Garden City Arena was due to open and teams were needed for the Niagara District Hockey League. The new team was called the Orioles. They were outfitted in dazzling orange sweaters with four black stripes on the arms. The letters T.S.T., for Toronto-St. Catharines Transport, fronted the jerseys in recognition of Touch Wood's trucking business. Players were driven in the back of one of his flatbed trucks to games against white teams in towns like St. Catharines, Niagara Falls and Guelph.

According to Hope Nicholson, "He always put a tarpaulin over the back so we didn't get too cold. But it was still chilly on the trips and in the games, which were often outdoors and sometimes in the locks of the Third Welland Canal."

The 16-member team was largely made up of the ancestors of Adam Nicholson, one of the community's founding members in the 1850s. Leverne Dorsey was only 16 when he started playing and recalled a team from Niagara-on-the-Lake. "They were all big farmer boys who used to hit hard, and we had a problem because not all of our fellows would come out and play. It wasn't uncommon for the Orioles to have only one extra player on the bench while the other teams were rolling two or three lines off their bench every three minutes." Recalling those days Dorsey claimed, "Teams we played treated us like any other team. Most of the racism I encountered came after hockey when I joined the army and later worked for myself."

A year later the team split up and the players joined various local clubs, suggesting that their original formation had less to do with discrimination than an opportunity to represent their community. The same could not be said for a *Toronto Telegram* reporter in 1937 who wrote, "They may not get anywhere as pucksters but the club suah [sic] has colah [sic]…yeah mam!"

Organizations like the OHA and its network of leagues were comparable to baseball's minor leagues in developing players. The above examples indicate, however, that unlike the all-encompassing policy of exclusion throughout all levels of organized baseball, the same did not apply in hockey. The pay and quality of play in senior hockey continued to be comparable or better than that found in the NHL.

The NHL's practices in matters of race, however, were more ambiguous and sinister in this regard. This was particularly true for a Black player in Ontario and Quebec's senior hockey leagues.

HERB CARNEGIE

In what is now the North York section of the expanded city of Toronto, the best Black player of his era, Herb Carnegie, played pond hockey with his brother Ossie. In the early 1930s he entered his first organized hockey competition at Lansing Public School. His Jamaican immigrant father cautioned him against his boyhood dream by telling him, "They won't let any Black boys in the National Hockey League."

Carnegie advanced through what was then the tough high school circuit of Toronto. He played junior hockey, practising regularly at Maple Leaf Gardens. One day his coach told him that the shadowy figure watching in the upper blues was the Toronto Maple Leafs' owner Conn Smythe. He was told that Smythe had indicated he'd sign Carnegie immediately if only someone could make him white.

Remembering the all-Black line. In the 1940s and 50s, Herbie and Ossie Carnegie and Manny McIntyre comprised what was then believed to be the only professional Black line combination ever. Though they never made the NHL, they dazzled everyone who saw them perform, *from left to right*: Ossie Carnegie, Herbie Carnegie and Manny McIntyre. *Courtesy of the Carnegie Family Collection.*

Carnegie has never forgotten the slight. It is a second-hand reference and, while others have corroborated the intent, Smythe did not publicly comment on the issue. Nor is there direct evidence that such a sentiment formed a part of official NHL policy.

Several interpretations are possible. At its root, Smythe's supposed suggestion that he would pay anyone $10,000 if he could turn Carnegie white is nonsensical. The intent may have been in the order of a joke—a cruel one, to be sure, but in keeping with the easy racism of the age. Or it may have had a more deadly intent—the NHL was determined to remain an all-white preserve like every other major league. We don't know.

The history of sports segregation had its roots in the backlash against full Black participation in public life following the American Civil War and particularly in the 1880s. It occurred before hockey's institutionalization.

Herb Carnegie wins Robert Abbott Memorial Trophy, Peterborough Golf and Country Club, July 26, 1971. He swung golf clubs with the same precision he brought to hockey. *Courtesy of the Carnegie Family Collection.*

By the time the NHL was established in 1917, the separation of the races in sports was an accepted reality. The decade of the NHL's founding was possibly the ugliest time for race relations in Canadian sports. Besides the banishment of Dick Brookins from the Western Canada Baseball League and the exclusion of Blacks from amateur boxing competition, there were extraordinary media representations of Blacks in Canadian newspapers. The *Toronto Daily Star* of May 1, 1914, for instance, had a cartoon in which an American ballplayer, Hub Perdue, is talking to a racially caricatured Black person with the caption, "Hub's greatest amusement is kiddin' the coons in the spring training camp."

Hockey owners of Carnegie's era grew up in this atmosphere. They were a particularly loathsome bunch of small-minded men despite the later eulogizing of their organizational role in hockey's early days. Their attitude, even to star players, was summed up in Smythe's comment to Harvey "Busher" Jackson who was seeking a $5,000 salary. "You'll take $4,000, or you won't play anywhere next year." Any challenge to the status quo was perceived as a threat. Hockey players were white Canadians exploited with low wages.

The only other comparable big league sport of the day, major league baseball, had a strict all-white practice. If baseball could exclude Blacks who clearly were the equal of, and in many cases better than, the existing talent pool of white players, hockey owners could easily rationalize their own behaviour.

Carnegie, however, was special—a great skater and goal scorer who won most valuable player awards in the superior Quebec Senior League from which Jean Beliveau graduated as did NHL legends Doug Harvey and Jacques Plante. Finally, in 1947, the New York Rangers invited him to their camp, but Carnegie had to negotiate his way up their farm system before being offered a contract to play on their best farm team in New Haven. Were the Rangers adopting the strategy of baseball's Brooklyn Dodgers who had made Jackie Robinson play a year of minor league ball before his Brooklyn debut? Did they want to see how Carnegie would do in their professional ranks? The record is unclear, but just the notion that a player like Carnegie, who was already playing in semi-pro leagues against white players, would now have to prove himself again against other white players in the Rangers' system, suggests the NHL was hoping Carnegie might forgo the opportunity.

And he did. Carnegie opted to return to senior hockey where the pay was better. In not following what might have been the Rangers overly cautious course of action, he played some part in *not* being the first Black in the NHL. However, he also lived in an economic climate which demanded decisions be made on factors other than history.

In retrospect it is clear that the league, run by narrow-minded men, missed an opportunity for leadership that a decision to put Carnegie in the NHL would have afforded. Black prospects were few and far between and no one could ever have subsequently claimed that the NHL had deliberately followed a policy of exclusion. Because of their tactics toward Carnegie, however, doubts about their practices are legitimate.

Carnegie might not have become a major star but he had much in common with perhaps 90 per cent of NHL players below that level. What separates any of them from a period of NHL play is often a matter of luck, happenstance, favouritism or, as in the case of Carnegie, imagination and open-mindedness—a commodity that the NHL lacked.

WILLIE O'REE

It was only a matter of time before a Black player made the NHL and, perhaps to the league's credit, the first such athlete was a career minor leaguer. Progressive baseball authorities (a minority themselves) feared that a mediocre performance by the first Black player would set the cause of integration back years. In hockey's case, it's more likely that its leaders were embarrassed that they alone among the big leagues in North America lacked racial variety.

Willie O'Ree, the first player of African ancestry in the National Hockey League.

The NHL's Black pioneer debuted in the city whose American League baseball team was the last to hire a Black player. Both events occurred around the same time. Willie O'Ree, dubbed the "King of the Near Miss" in a *Hockey Pictorial* profile in 1964, played his first game for the Boston Bruins on January 18, 1958. His near-miss label described an inability to put the puck in the net despite great speed, which presented him with many scoring opportunities. O'Ree's ultimate ability, however, had been forever compromised by a devastating eye injury a few seasons before. He kept that information to himself.

He was born in Fredericton, New Brunswick, in 1935, the youngest of 14 children, many of whom excelled in sports. His brother, Leon, was a professional football player; his brother, Richard, a Maritime boxing champ; and two of his sisters played basketball and softball. O'Ree was a good baseball player but his real love was hockey. He played junior hockey in Kitchener before graduating to Quebec's minor league pro team.

O'Ree was never an NHL standout. He managed only four goals in 45 games over two seasons. Still, he had a long career particularly with the Los Angeles Blades of the Western Hockey League in the 1960s. O'Ree said, "They've called me the Jackie Robinson of Hockey, and I'm aware of being the first, and of the responsibilities, but I'm also aware that there have not been and are not many colored players able to play hockey, that there has never been the discrimination in this game there was in baseball, and that I didn't face any of the very real problems Robinson had to face."

In a later video documentary produced on his life, O'Ree did recall a damaged right eye which restricted his playing ability and, more seriously, ugly incidents such as the racial taunting by Chicago Black Hawks player, Eric Nesterenko, who also butt-ended him in the mouth. It led to a fight and a vicious reaction from Chicago fans, shocked that a Black man would retaliate.

Other Black players of this era included Willie O'Ree's Los Angeles teammate in the sixties, Stan Maxwell. Another lone pioneer was Arthur Dorrington who signed with the Atlantic City Seagulls of the Eastern Amateur League in 1950. A year later Dorrington joined the New Haven Tomahawks of the professional Eastern Hockey League for a game against the Washington Lions on November 16. The Baltimore Afro-American newspaper suggested that he was possibly "the first colored ice hockey player to compete professionally in the United States."

A few weeks later, George Lyle Jr., writing in the same paper, said, "This week I took in my first ice hockey game and it's all that advance notices have called for. It's positively the fastest game I've ever witnessed and the fact that Art Dorrington, a lad from Truro, Nova Scotia, was on the team made it even more interesting.

"Dorrington, the colored player in the Eastern Hockey league is 21, weighs 160 and skates like a streak. Last year he played with the Atlantic

City Seagulls and started the season with New Haven Tomahawks. His debut with the Washington Lions last week was impressive...."

At hockey's amateur levels meanwhile, Black players like John Utendale played alongside Mark Messier's father, Doug, on the junior Edmonton Oil Kings. They went to the Western Canada finals in 1957. Utendale later played for the University of British Columbia.

THE CONTEMPORARY SCENE

Two things were required before Black players would enter the NHL in significant numbers. One was the growth of Canada's Black population. It expanded the pool of qualified players. A second factor was NHL expansion. As the number of jobs grew so have opportunities for players once consigned to minor league status or ignored all together.

There was a long hiatus after O'Ree's brief NHL career. Mike Marson finally played 196 NHL games beginning in 1974. Tony McKegney was the first Black NHL player to establish a significant career. A family in Sarnia had adopted him at the age of one. He learned to play in the town's local system. "Sometimes I would wonder why I was trying to be a pro player when there no one like me to look up to. I'm proud of the fact that I was the first Black to establish myself in the NHL [debuting in 1978]. I hope that helps youngsters who need someone to emulate." With nearly 350 NHL regular season and playoff goals, including a 40-goal season in 1987–88 with the St. Louis Blues, McKegney became a bona fide star.

The most successful Black hockey player was Grant Fuhr from Spruce Grove, Alberta. He was the number one goalie for much of the Edmonton Oilers' Stanley Cup dynasty years of the 1980s, when their extraordinary lineup included Wayne Gretzky, Mark Messier, Paul Coffey and Jari Kurri.

Fuhr's teammates called him, "Cocoa," in the context of dressing room camaraderie. Gretzky's biography cites an instance in which they gave Fuhr some white shoe polish for use under his eyes to deflect the sun's rays during a charitable softball game. All the white players of course used lampblack. It was the irreverent stuff of team solidarity. Gretzky expressed pride that Fuhr was the first Black to have his name on the Stanley Cup. He has also been inducted into the Hockey Hall of Fame.

Other notable pioneers include John Paris from Windsor, Nova Scotia, the first Black head coach in professional hockey. He led the Atlanta

Knights to the International Hockey League championship in 1994.

Angela James, the child of a Black father, was the premier women's hockey player in the world during the game's revival in the 1980s and 1990s as it sought Olympic Games recognition. She played hockey as a child on neighbourhood boys' teams until other parents objected to a girl outshining their children. She bussed, with her mother, to outlying rinks at all hours of the night just to get playing time with other girls. She graduated to more competitive senior women's hockey and was a member of several Canadian world championship teams.

James was cruelly cut from the national team on the eve of the 1998 Winter Olympics, a decision with no apparent racial overtones. Canada failed to win gold at those games as much because of the loss of her ability to irritate rivals and score crucial goals.

Hilton Ruggles from Montreal was a pathfinder overseas. He was the first Black import to make a major impact in British hockey. Ruggles led Manchester Storm in scoring with 18 goals in the team's 42-game schedule in 1996–97. Crowds averaged over 9,000 a game. He also had played for Whitley, Solihull, Murrayfield and Cardiff. He listed his nickname as "Homie" and said his ultimate ambition was to be the "First Black hockey player to play on Mars."

Anson Carter has been a member of two World Hockey championship teams and he has perhaps the most famous goal by a Black hockey player, scoring the winning tally in the 2003 final. His parents were both natives of Barbados, coming to Canada, as part of the great immigration boom. At first they attempted to discourage his hockey career because they said the sport was too rough. He eventually surpassed his Scarborough mates in skating ability. Carter had a university career with the Michigan State University Spartans and was a member of Canada's 1994 World Junior champs.

Two other prominent athletes, National Football League player Tommy Kane from Montreal and baseball's Fergie Jenkins were promising hockey players in Canada but chose to play in the two leading sports of the United States.

RECENT INDIGNITIES AND OPPORTUNITIES

Overt racism of the kind Jackie Robinson experienced in the forties seemed to have disappeared from the modern sporting scene, but in the 1997–98 season several Black players were subject to racial taunts.

Chris Simon called Mike Grier, of the Edmonton Oilers, a "nigger." It is the word with the harshest slave and Jim Crow connotations and for which there is zero tolerance when used in such a defamatory context. Grier, an American Black and son of a National Football League administrator, had worked as a volunteer in the "Hockey in Harlem" program that brought the game to underprivileged children in New York. Neither he nor others could understand why Simon, an Ojibway native from Wawa, Ontario, would be so insensitive to another minority person in the NHL. "That's what was strange to me, that it was someone who has his background and his race," Grier said. In any case Simon, who apologized directly to Grier, was briefly suspended.

Tony McKegney was befuddled by Simon's comments, "Why should the colour factor enter into it? That always troubled me." McKegney recalled playing in Chicago where he was probably the only Black person in the entire arena of 20,000 people. "A lot of people have never been faced with that type of difficulty or awareness. They miss the whole concept of what it's like to be the minority in a situation like that and the psychological setup you have to put yourself through going out on the ice night after night and the opposing teams are calling you whatever, and the guys are spitting in your face and then you're dealing with whatever goes on in the dressing room with your teammates." He said he had never experienced such behaviour playing kids hockey in Scarborough.

The incident raised questions about organized hockey's commitment to racial fairness. Shortly thereafter the *Toronto Star* reported that referee Carl Friday of the Metro Toronto Hockey League had experienced racial slurs and threats from a 16 year-old hockey player.

Herbie Carnegie recalled, "I never experienced any incidents in the game of hockey from other players. The fans were another thing but I don't call that an incident in hockey. That was their own ignorance..."

His grandson, Rane Carnegie, said "I think my grandfather should have been able to play in the National Hockey League but he couldn't because of the racism back then. I want to do what my grandpa couldn't do." Rane played for the Belleville Bulls in Ontario's Major Junior League and was invited to the Toronto Maple Leafs' training camp in the fall of 2003.

For a brief period Black players seemed to be cast in the role of their team's enforcer, such as Donald Brashear, Georges Laraque and Peter Worrell. Even that characterization has faded following Jarome Iginla's superstar season of 2001–02. The Calgary Flames player led the NHL in

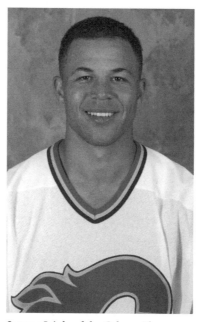

Jarome Iginla of the Calgary Flames, 2004 Stanley Cup Finalists. He had two goals and an assist against Slovakia in leading Canada into the 2004 World Cup of Hockey semi-finals, a tournament that Canada eventually won. *Courtesy of the Hockey Hall of Fame.*

goals, was awarded the Maurice Richard Trophy, finished second in MVP voting and helped Canada win gold at the 2002 Winter Olympics. Iginla's last name means "big tree" in the Yoruba Nigerian language of his father.

By the time Iginla captained the Calgary Flames to the Stanley Cup finals in 2004, he was being acknowledged as the best player in the NHL for his on-ice leadership, ability to score goals in crucial situations and hold his own when the going got tough.

The underlying itch of racism in hockey, however, refuses to disappear completely. A junior hockey coach, John Vanbiesbrouck of the Sault Greyhounds, lost his job in the 2002–03 season after repeatedly slurring his defenceman Trevor Daley with the same language that got Chris Simon suspended. Whether it came from malice, stupidity or ignorance, such behaviour, which once savaged Willie O'Ree in Chicago over forty years before, was no longer tolerated in the game's circles.

12

VISITING HEROES

CANADA'S BLACK POPULATION WAS, until very recently, almost invisible. Mainstream Canadians could smugly assert a fairminded superiority over their white American neighbours. Their first encounter with the Black community was often through the lives of visiting sports figures or entertainers. This has changed in the last 30 years.

Black Canadians, along with immigrants from around the world, have expanded the choices available to Canadians in entertainment, food, business opportunity and daily play and recreation. This is reflected in a revitalized interest and participation in games like cricket and soccer.

In sports, Canadians have generally let a person's performance speak for itself. For this reason the opportunity for Black athletes to assume not only team leadership positions but also managing roles has had little of the anxiety that Americans express. The 1990s saw the first World Series victory for a Black baseball manager as the Toronto Blue Jays won consecutive titles in 1992 and 1993. Yet that particular feature raised so little comment in Canada that manager Cito Gaston himself had to continually remind people of its significance. Black quarterbacks were still considered noteworthy in the National Football League long after their presence on Canadian fields was taken for granted. American Warren Moon made his fame in Canada with the Edmonton Eskimos before joining the Houston Oilers.

Foreign Black athletes are not a recent phenomenon. American boxer Jack Johnson, who became heavyweight champion in 1908, was among the first to find Canada a refuge from the severe restrictions of his own country.

When Johnson was freed on bail in the United States for "taking a [willing] white woman across state lines for immoral purposes," he disguised himself as a member of a Black barnstorming baseball team, the Chicago American Giants, and crossed into Canada with the team. Despite his fame, customs

Top, Clarence "Cito" Gaston, a former American player, won two World Series as field manager of the Toronto Blue Jays; *below,* the first Toronto Raptors general manager, Isiah Thomas. *Courtesy of Seneca College.*

officials failed to recognize him. In this case, at least, a Black person's anonymity within the mainstream society had worked to his advantage. Once in Canada, he jumped bail and pursued his career outside the United States.

During the integration of organized baseball in the 1940s, major league teams often sent their new recruits to Canadian minor league teams. The reception was even-handed in contrast to many American towns, which openly abused these players. Sam Bankhead became the first Black manager in organized baseball in 1950 with the Pittsburgh Pirates farm team in Farnham, Quebec, of the Class A Provincial League.

The Canadian Football League survived the post-war popularity of the National Football League by providing opportunities for minorities to assume leadership positions. American Black, George Reed, a great running back with the Saskatchewan Roughriders in the 1960s, played an important role as a player representative and union organizer.

In the 1970s, the fledgling game of soccer received a boost with the on-field leadership of Black Portuguese star Eusebio. He led the Toronto Metros-Croatia to the North American soccer title in 1976.

In two major American-based sports leagues, baseball and basketball, the Black athlete was a role model and hero for Canadians of all generations.

American George Reed found football fame and a future career in Canada as running back for the Saskatchewan Roughriders. *Courtesy of Canada's Sports Hall of Fame.*

THE TORONTO BLUE JAYS

The Blue Jays entered baseball's American League in 1977. They became one of that sport's great success stories, quickly becoming Canada's baseball team. The Jays had 11 straight winning seasons beginning in 1983, culminating in back-to-back World Series triumphs in 1992 and '93. They regularly attracted over four million fans a year. They were one of the first teams to exploit the talent base of the Dominican Republic. Early stars included 1987 American League Most Valuable Player George Bell and shortstop Tony Fernandez who played for the Jays on three different occasions.

After a stumbling start in 1989, the Jays promoted their hitting coach, Clarence "Cito" Gaston, to field manager. Placing his faith in veteran players and relying on them as role models, he guided the team to a divisional pennant.

After a disappointing 1990 season, the team traded for Joe Carter, an American born in Oklahoma City, and Robbie Alomar, a gifted second baseman from a baseball family in Puerto Rico. These two players proved the catalyst for the Jays' eventual world titles.

George Bell from the Dominican Republic was American League Most Valuable Player in 1987 as a member of the Toronto Blue Jays. *Courtesy of the Toronto Blue Jays.*

In 1992 they were supported by, among others, the St. Paul, Minnesota native, Dave Winfield, who drove in the winning runs against the Atlanta Braves. Joe Carter hit one of the most dramatic homeruns in baseball history a year later, winning the World Series over the Philadelphia Phillies. Dave Stewart from Oakland, California, led the team's pitching staff. He entered Toronto sporting lore by serving meals to the homeless on the Canadian Thanksgiving prior to his playoff appearances.

The Blue Jays had losing seasons thereafter and Cito Gaston's relationship with the local Toronto media became strained. He finally accused them of racism for their criticisms during the 1997 season,

Left, Joe Carter. His game six home run in the bottom of the ninth inning of the 1993 World Series brought a second title to the Toronto Blue Jays; *right*, Roberto "Robbie" Alomar's all-star seasons in Toronto, as part of two World Series winners, put the second baseman in line for eventual entry into baseball's hall of fame in Cooperstown. *Both photographs courtesy of the Toronto Blue Jays.*

though he could cite no incidents. Many Black Canadians were sympathetic to the manager but his departure during the last week of the season elicited no protest, perhaps because the team's woeful performance over the past four seasons had muted even Cito's strongest supporters.

MIKE "PINBALL" CLEMONS

Few players have had such a marked impact on their league as Mike Clemons of the Toronto Argonaut football club of the Canadian Football League (CFL). An American import from William and Mary College in 1989, he played on three Grey Cup champion teams.

He promoted the beleaguered league on radio sports shows and regularly participated in community charity events. In a city gifted with major league

Michael "Pinball" Clemons, originally from Florida, had a brilliant CFL career with the Toronto Argonauts that saw him establish a world record for most career all-purpose yards by a professional football player with 25,396 yards. Clemons has done it all with the Argos, as player, coach and club executive. Today in Toronto, he is well-known for his ongoing involvement with charities, schools and other community groups. *Courtesy of the Toronto Argonauts Football Club.*

hockey, baseball and basketball teams, it was a player from a sport, which played second fiddle to the National Football League, who maintained the greatest community profile.

Whether it was returning kicks for touchdowns or taking passes from quarterback Doug Flutie, Clemons' field presence made possible two consecutive Grey Cup victories for the Argonauts in 1996 and 1997. His last minute touchdown against Montreal in 1997 broke a 30-30 tie and saved the team from an embarrassing upset at home. It sent them to the Grey Cup finals.

After one charity promotion with the Canadian Legion a member said, "I've seen you on TV so many times and it seems that anytime there's something on about keeping kids out of trouble you're the one I see talking. It makes lots of other people ashamed to be Canadians because you're American and you do so much up here."

For his part Clemons said, "Toronto is my home. I love it here. When they ask me what is keeping us [his family] here, I say it's the people. They make the difference. They have a tolerance for race relations."

Clemons celebrated Black History Month in 2004 by appearing at a public meeting with four other former Black CFL players who also stayed in Canada after their careers had finished. One of these, Ulysses Curtis, taught school in Toronto for over 30 years following his football career with the Argonauts from 1950–54.

Curtis came to Canada after his All-American career at Florida A & M. He remembered the Toronto of 1950 as friendly but with undertones of racism. "Montreal, Calgary and Winnipeg had already had Black players and it took Toronto a few years to come along," he said.

Another athlete recognized along with Clemons and Curtis was Chuck Ealey, a financial advisor in Brampton. He recalled being undrafted by the NFL and coming to Canada where he led Hamilton to the 1972 Grey Cup.

Ealey said, "Toronto is a very diverse city; you can live where you want and go where you want without trouble."

13

INTO THE FUTURE

OVER THE LAST TWO CENTURIES sport has moved from the fringes of popular culture to a central place in defining lifestyles, public interest and private investment. The military-industrial complex might have more power, but today it is the global sports and entertainment business that shapes personal and national perceptions.

Athletes like Michael Jordan, Muhammad Ali, and Pele have become arguably the best-known people in the world. All are Black and this has led to the suggestion that Black achievement is too narrowly focused on the sports arena. On the other hand, such claims may unfairly taint accomplishments that, in the cases of the three athletes above, have extended far beyond sports.

Organized professional sport remains an incomplete area of Black participation, however, because of the disproportionately small number of Black managers, owners, administrators and entrepreneurs.

At its root, this narrowing of opportunity reflects a larger public problem—the inability to recognize continuing features of past oppression and false stereotypes. Canadians, to their credit, have played a role in responding to issues and broadening opportunities. They were leaders in the international movement banning South African participation in sports while that country's government followed a policy of internal apartheid. Even professional golfers from South Africa were prohibited from participating in Canada. Sports bodies were told their federal funds would be withdrawn if athletes competed against South Africa. Canada helped show the world that the sports field was not immune from political and moral issues.

The Canadian Football League (CFL) was a leader in hiring Black quarterbacks long before the National Football League (NFL). Warren Moon

Frank Baines of Central Tech finishes the 100-yard distance in 9.9 seconds, 1962. *Courtesy of Canadian Sports Hall of Fame.*

won five Grey Cups before opting to return to the United States. The CFL has also been more aggressive than the NFL in giving Black head coaches an opportunity.

As well, African-Canadian athletes have not been constrained from entering sports in which they had traditionally not competed. As far back as the late 1950s, Ivan Stewart had been a pioneer Black player in lacrosse as a member of a Mann Cup team, the New Westminster Salmonbellies. More recently, gymnast Curtis Hibbert was a two-time medallist at the world championships.

Black Canadians have also achieved prominence in American-based sports in which they had not previously been represented. In the nineties, Jamaal Magloire, a graduate of Toronto's Eastern Commerce High School, played at the University of Kentucky and Toronto's Michael Meeks at Canisius University. They are part of a new generation of Canadian Blacks invading what once was an almost solely American preserve within the National Collegiate Athletic Association's (NCAA) college basketball ranks. Of the 59 foreign countries represented on teams in Division 1 of the NCAA in 1997, the 43 Canadians surpassed by over three times the next best represented country.

When he was asked prior to Kentucky's NCAA championship season of 1997–98 if, like many former Kentucky players, he envisioned residing in Lexington after his college days, Jamaal Magloire replied, "Home is home. I'll go back to Toronto." He became an NBA star known for his willingness to wear down opponents physically by laying on the body. In 2004 he was the second Canadian (Steve Nash was the first) selected to play in the NBA All-Star game.

The naming of facilities like the Harry Jerome Sports Centre built as a full-time indoor velodrome in Burnaby, British Columbia, indicated a

Andre Dawson starred for the Montreal Expos in their glory years of the late 1970s and early 1980s. He was inducted into Canada's Baseball Hall of Fame in 2004. *Courtesy of the Montreal Expos.*

Canadian interest in recognizing past achievement as well.

Inconsistencies have been part of Canadian history, but today Black athletes are often more likely to experience ugly racial incidents outside Canada. Such was the case for Brampton's Jason Bent and Scarborough's Dwayne de Rosario, two Canadian-born Black soccer players who retained their family love for Caribbean spices and sported West Indian dreadlocks. Hired in 1997 to play professional soccer in the former East Germany, they were subject to direct racial harassment from teammates, fans and locals in the street.

In several areas, however, disquieting undercurrents of past injustice remain. Blacks are often shunted into narrow, even dead-end, education streams at the same time they are expected to be school sports leaders. While this problem is more extreme in the United States, it remains an issue that Canadians cannot ignore.

White Canadians have often been critical of their country's immigration policies, which have seen Canada's Black population grow to around a million, with over 70 per cent of them living in Toronto and Montreal. Highly publicized encounters with the judicial system have painted a distorted picture of the community particularly when it is often young Black men who are victims. In 2003, 29 of 31 persons killed by guns in Toronto were described as either Black or Central/East Asian. Even leaders in the Black community, while citing an absence of jobs and family breakdown as factors, remain perplexed as to an ultimate solution.

Blacks are more likely to be the victims of racial profiling such as that experienced by boxer Kirk Johnson in 1998 when his car, with Texas license plates, was stopped in his home province of Nova Scotia. A lengthy human rights hearing ruled that Halifax police had discriminated against him when they ticketed and seized his car.

These incidents have occurred alongside the continuing influx of West Indian immigrants who have done so much to raise Canada's sporting profile. Athletes of colour in recent years have included immigrants from

all parts of the world. David Defiagbon, an immigrant from Nigeria, settled in Halifax and won a boxing silver medal for Canada at the 1996
Olympics. He represented what until then had been relatively rare in Canadian sports, an African-Canadian athlete who was actually born in Africa.

Daniel Igali is the most prominent African immigrant. He competed
in wrestling for Nigeria at the 1994 Commonwealth Games in Victoria,
British Columbia, and then chose to stay, fearing a precarious existence
in his military-ruled country. He struggled to build a successful career
in a new land obviously foreign to his life experience. He shared an apartment with some less committed athletes who partied too often for his
liking. He worked nights as a security guard and sometimes only slept a
few hours before practice. At the Sydney Summer Olympics in 2000 he
won the gold and then placed the Canadian flag on the mat, jogged around
it and knelt down to kiss it.

Other African and South Asian refugees and immigrants from Africa have
contributed in other ways, raising the profile of games like soccer and cricket.
Ethiopian and Somali soccer teams quietly play on the apparent fringes of
Canadian sport in large public parks in Toronto, Montreal, Victoria and elsewhere. They wrestle with old country rivalries. In the case of the Ethiopian
community, even the club's name was contentious, the original Blue Nile
reflecting the northern part of Ethiopia and one not favoured by those from
the eastern part. Eventually they settled on the Ethio-Stars sports club.

Somalians, also fleeing war in their country, likewise developed an
ambitious soccer program on Toronto's Eglinton Flats at Jane and Eglinton Avenues. Three students from the University of Toronto established
a league in 1992. The players' Muslim heritage was acknowledged in the
enforcement of rules prohibiting rough play and cursing. It also had to
wrestle with old Somali tribal rivalries at different stages of its evolution.
Both Somalians and Ethiopians have participated in more extensive North
American gatherings of soccer teams representing their communities in
the large cities of the United States and Canada.

People of colour now include immigrants from India, Pakistan and
Sri Lanka. They have popularized the game of cricket. Graduates of Marc
Garneau Collegiate in Toronto formed the Cambridge Cricket Club in
1997. The club had links to the city's growing Sri Lankan community.

Clubs like this were the foundation for the renewal of a game that had
been Canada's major sport in the early 19th century. The world's first ever
international match was between Canada and the United States in 1844.

By the 1870s, however, cricket had become a minor sport. It remained that way until the arrival of immigrants from cricket-playing countries. The country's national cricket team, playing in the game's World Cup in 2003, was a picture of the new Canada. Players included Sanjayan Thuraisingam born in Ceylon in 1969, a powerfully built fast-medium bowler credited with taking the important wickets that helped Canada qualify for the World Cup. The bowling of Austin Codrington, born in Jamaica in 1975, keyed Canada's upset victory of Bangladesh at the World Cup.

It may be some time before the current globalization of living places and the growing multiracial face of youth (what the *New York Times,* December 28, 2003, called "Generation Ethnically Ambiguous") remove the last vestiges of discrimination. We are finally at a time, however, when sporting distinction based on race is fading in importance.

American basketball player Rasheed Wallace attacked the National Basketball Association commissioner for acting like a white establishment landlord exploiting Black youths. He was criticized by a former Black college coach, John Thompson, who said, "What Rasheed is doing is attacking an old scar where it doesn't exist."

Basketball, a game until recently dominated by Black Americans, represents a post-modern development in sports. The country of origin of basketball players now ranges from Africa to Eastern Europe and China, reflecting the globalization of employment opportunities for gifted performers. Talent, whether it is athletes or computer designers, can pick where it lives and works. Boxer Lennox Lewis chose to represent Great Britain whose colours he wore in winning the Heavyweight Championship of the World, but he continues to spend considerable time in Canada. Ben Johnson may have been disgraced for his 1988 misadventure, but still feels comfortable in Canada. Mark McKoy left Canada for Austria after winning a gold medal, but later returned.

Jockey Patrick Husbands upon arrival in Canada said, "I want to win every major race here. He went on to claim the Queen's Plate aboard Wando. *Courtesy of Woodbine Entertainment.*

Athletes come to Canada for the same reason that others, who grew up in Canada, go elsewhere—opportunity. One such was Patrick Husbands, a proud Bajan, who achieved everything available to him in Barbados. His family were renowned local jockeys—father Walter in the late fifties and sixties and his brothers Anthony and Simon.

"Simon wanted me to come here with my 'bug,' but I enjoyed Barbados. I was the talk of the town, so I couldn't leave. But there was really nothing more for me there. I had won the championship and was the leading rider. In 1993 I finally came here."

At first no one knew him. He tried the Fort Erie track but couldn't get any rides. Finally, he picked up a few up at Woodbine. His Canadian career had begun. Ten years later he became part of Canadian horse racing history, riding Wando to the Canadian Triple Crown. He said, "I achieved the three big races I really wanted to win in my whole riding career." Included in those was the Queen's Plate, arguably one of the most famous races in the world.

The stories about contemporary Black athletes are not those of victims, but people freely choosing their own identity.

BIGUP

Against the historic background of sports' tumultuous entanglement in matters of race, Shondell Brooks and Roland Lewis shared, at Toronto's North Beach in 1994, a common dream. Their vision was a testament to the new forms of leadership, identity and freedom to define their own direction, emerging within the Black sports community.

"We wanted to form an all-Black volleyball team," Brooks said, "not to exclude anybody but to create some positive role models for our community. We noticed that other ethnic and national groups weren't uncomfortable with teams representing them—in fact it seemed a matter of pride and a focus for sporting interest.

"But we had other goals as well. We wanted to dispel some myths about the Black volleyballer. We weren't just good shooters who couldn't dig out a ball or make a good pass. I'd been in games where the other team openly told each other to serve it to the Black guy. That's how little respect there was."

Roland Lewis talked about their hope of appealing to a new generation of young Blacks. "So many kids focus on basketball. I've heard them

The volleyball team BigUp, *left to right*: Marc Roberts, Mike Cameron, Clayton Carim-bocas, Shondell Brooks, Paul Carter, Ryan McNeil, Ishmael Joseph, Delroy Rhooms, Andrew White, Dwight David, Jimmy Timm, and (seated) Roland Lewis.

say that volleyball is a sissy sport lacking body contact. But I just love the game and wanted to communicate that feeling. This game surpasses everything. It even comes between relationships."

Theirs was a Black Canadian dream. Shondell Brooks's family could be traced back to the earliest Black settlement in Nova Scotia 200 years ago. They had a street named after them in the East Preston district of Halifax. As for Lewis, he experienced both of Canada's language solitudes having been born in Montreal and growing up in Toronto.

Despite Brooks and Lewis's noble idea they were entering territory well worn with history and pre-conceived impressions. Given that today large numbers of Black and white players play volleyball together, the conscious formation of an all-Black team seemed to recall the days when segregated teams were mandated by the majority white population.

"It kind of hurt," said Brooks, "when players on other teams would question our all-Black lineup and suggest that because they were white they wouldn't be welcome on the team. Some wondered if we weren't just practising a kind of reverse racism.

"But we really felt that we, as Black players, had something to prove and this was the only way it could be done. Later, and I guess once we were secure with our image, we welcomed white players, and also had a player of Chinese background."

Lewis said, "All we were pushing for was a Black identity. I've experienced racism throughout my life but it hasn't brought me down. I wasn't interested in reverse discrimination. We wanted to create a bond, build our community."

When they gathered in the fall of 1994 in a high school gym, their numbers included some of volleyball's leading players. One of them, Marc Roberts, recalled with delight the scene that greeted him. "I remember walking in the gym and just being astounded, I couldn't believe that there were all these talented Black players from so many different cultures and backgrounds.

"There must have been 40 or 50 and they were from all over, Canadian-born, American, Guyanese, Jamaican. It was amazing. Socially there was a connection between us and when playing we seemed to have this unconscious level of communication."

Ishmael Joseph suggested the team name BigUp—a casual slang expression often used by disc jockeys as a greeting. As a new team, the Ontario Volleyball Association placed them in its "C" division. It was soon obvious that they were far superior to potential rivals, so they were bumped to "B" and then won a realignment qualifier to leap up to the "A" level.

"I won't pretend we always got along," Brooks recalled. "We had some real prima-donnas, and confrontational players who turned off other guys who might have joined the team. Most of our team members were go-to guys on their previous squad and now they had to share the spotlight. A lot of Black players like the power position, but that may be because that's the role we have always been assigned. In my experience not many of us seem to be skilled setters." In volleyball, Black players have often been stereotyped in certain positions. Exceptions to that rule were often discouraged or dropped from a team.

Through their first winter BigUp gradually jelled, becoming a cohesive team with different players taking turns being their go-to-guy. They entered the Ontario playoffs leading to the National Senior Men's A Championship. "The provincials were actually tougher than the nationals," Brooks said. "In the record books, because we often won two straight, it may appear to have been easy but it wasn't.

"My strongest memory at the nationals was a chippy match with Quebec. There was a play in which one of our guys, Clayton Carimbocas, may have contacted one of their blockers. "Stix" as we call him spikes straight down. They started yapping at us but picked the wrong guy in "Stix." He's a guy with an attitude!

"We assumed the comments weren't very flattering but couldn't tell because they were all in French. But from that point on we just demolished them. I think they scored two points from then on. They picked the wrong team to flair up!"

Representing Ontario, BigUp played Newfoundland in the finals. Their confidence and satisfaction at coming so far in one season built as the game neared the end. "I was used to losing," Lewis says, "but for those last few points I smelled victory in the air. I was overcome with excitement. It was like nothing I've ever felt before. It was so intense that feeling of knowing you're going to win. Everything was coming out right and I gave a little thought to our success in overcoming the stereotypes and the impression that we'd choke."

"We never verbally hammered our identity at anyone," said Brooks. "We just wanted to play and be respected as Black athletes who can master all the positions."

In 1995–96 the team jumped to the "AA" level, created another team to play senior men's A and welcomed the remnants of an all-Black female team from the previous season. With three teams, BigUp was an organization to be reckoned with, but it couldn't attract sufficient sponsorship. Many of its players were raising children. They couldn't afford the cost and time required for travel and uniforms. Reluctantly, at season end they folded.

BASEBALL TODAY

In 1997, on the 50th anniversary of Robinson's reintegration of major league baseball, there were concerns about the continuing abandonment of baseball by young Black athletes in the United States. In Canada the reverse has been true, largely because of the growth in the Black population resulting from recent immigration.

The Walcott Brothers, (Richie, Sheldon and Kenny) played senior baseball for the Sydney Sooners in the Nova Scotia Senior Baseball League in the early 1990s. Kenny also played football with the Ottawa Rough Riders of the Canadian Football League while Richie was also a professional hockey player with the Baltimore Skipjacks of the American Hockey League.

Among the notable athletes who made the major leagues was Nigel Wilson, born in Oshawa in 1970 and raised in Ajax where he played high school volleyball and basketball. As a baseball player, however, he was named to Canada's National Youth team in 1987 and by 1992 he had become the 7th Canadian placed on the Toronto Blue Jays 40-man roster.

The next year, however, he was the first player selected in the expansion draft by the Florida Marlins where he failed to develop as quickly as they wished. Florida's strategy gradually changed from developing young players to spending huge sums on established stars. They were rewarded with a World Series title by 1997.

Nigel Wilson from Ajax, Ontario, playing for the minor league Edmonton Trappers baseball team.

Wilson, however, followed in the path of another Black Canadian and former Blue Jay, Toronto-born Rob Ducey, by playing baseball in Japan. In 1997, Wilson led the Japanese Pacific League in home runs (37) in the first of a two-year contract with the Nippon Ham Fighters. As for Ducey, the former high school wrestler in Cambridge, Ontario, played outfield through the 2001 season.

Others like Hugh Walters demonstrated that for the majority of Canadian Blacks the route to success was through the traditional educational and career path. Scouted as a baseball player in his youth and a scholarship candidate for American colleges, he eventually opted for a teaching career in Ontario.

Nevertheless, by 2004 he had become a significant symbol of the emerging role of the Black sports leader. He coached within a successful volleyball organization, the Ganaraska Wolves, east of Toronto. Many of its graduates went on to successful university careers. As well, Walters operated an annual summer Academy Baseball School for children in Whitby, Ontario.

CHARMAINE HOOPER

The Hooper family immigrated to Canada from Georgetown, Guyana. Lyndon was a national soccer team member for over ten years beginning in 1986. He scored one of Canada's five goals in his second game against Malaysia. His long-standing teammates have included Guyanese-born Alex Bunbury and Randy Samuel, born in Trinidad and Tobago.

Lyndon's sister Charmaine emerged as one of Canada's leading female soccer players winning recognition as the country's top female player in 1994 and 1995. For a time, as a member of Tokyo Shidax, she was the

Left, Charmaine Hooper: "I'm not out there to be liked. I'm out there to win. If I intimidate opponents because I never quit and I battle for every ball, then that's OK." *Above*, Charmaine Hooper: "I've always had people complain about my physical play for as long as I remember, so I've never really been bothered by that." *Both photographs courtesy of Ontario Soccer Association.*

only female among over 40 Canadians who were playing professional soccer outside Canada.

Charmaine and her older brother also established a soccer skills academy to train the next generation of soccer players in their hometown of Ottawa. In 2003 Hooper led her Canadian teammates to the semi-finals of the World Cup of soccer for women.

PERDITA FELICIEN

The Canadian winner of the 100 metre hurdles at the World Athletics Championships in Paris in the summer of 2003 was largely unknown at the time to the Canadian public. Victory made Perdita Felicien a favourite to win gold at the 2004 Summer Olympics, but unfortunately she would trip on the first hurdle in the finals and not finish the race. "It was my race to win and I lost it," she said afterwards. Felicien apologized to the Canadian public but, because of her accomplishments up to that time, no one felt this was necessary.

Perdita Felicien, a true champion. She called her 2004 Olympic fall her worst nightmare come true, but immediately began planning for 2008 in Beijing. *Courtesy of Nike Canada Ltd.*

Perdita Felicien was born in Oshawa in 1980 and grew up in Pickering, Ontario. As a child she competed once a year in her elementary school's track meet. She didn't run the hurdles seriously until grade 11. She was high school champion in 1998, Canadian junior champ a year later, and Canadian champion in 2000. Felicien's potential was realized at the University of Illinois where she obtained All-American status, was named the Drake Relays' Most Outstanding Athlete in 2002, and was the Big Ten Champion in the 100 metre hurdles in 2003.

She had been eliminated early in the 2000 Olympics and began working on her starts, considered to be her weakness. This was the final piece she needed. Perdita's great start in the Paris finals allowed her to maintain the lead to the finish line.

Felicien was named Canada's female athlete of the year in 2003 and described the tremendous pride she felt every time she returned to Canada after competing internationally.

EPILOGUE

I T SOMETIMES APPEARS THAT public attention to matters of race has never been more pronounced than it is today. In many ways that discussion is a refreshing willingness to confront age-old stereotypes and injustices.

Its very openness is necessarily uncomfortable for it recovers unpleasant memories and, at the same time, requires public policy initiatives to ensure equitable opportunity. Yet in the longer perspective, such talk and action brings us closer to a time when items of race have lost their importance. Until such time, we revisit the past as both a guide and a rationale for aggressive public action.

In so many cases the next generation of leaders are already assuming new roles in society. They are proclaiming a national identity that pays little attention to race and everything to demonstrated ability.

Sources

PART ONE

1: THE BLACK EXPERIENCE IN CANADA

Two major sources for this chapter, and informing the understanding of the African-Canadian experience in Canada, are: *The Blacks in Canada: A History* by Robin W. Winks (New Haven: Yale University Press, 1971); and *Towards Freedom: The African-Canadian Experience* by Ken Alexander and Avis Glaze (Toronto: Umbrella Press, 1996). Other sources include: *An Enduring Heritage: Black Contributions to Early Ontario* (Toronto: Dundurn Press Limited, 1984); "Canadian People of African Descent: Significant Dates" by Rosemary Sadlier, Ontario Black History Society, from www.black-web.com; *Black Like Who?* by Rinaldo Walcott (Toronto: Insomniac Press, 1997); "What an African-Canadian is" by Graham Fraser, *Globe and Mail*, August 30, 1997.

2: THE SPORTING SCENE

Among the sources supporting observations in this chapter are: *Darwin's Athletes: How Sport has Damaged Black America and Preserved the Myth of Race* by John Hoberman (Boston: Houghton Mifflin, 1997); "Broken Hoop Dreams for the Basketball Players of Coney Island" by Brent Staples, *New York Times*, February 1, 2004; "Are Pro Sports Bad for Black America?" from *U.S. News and World Report* special issue, March 24, 1997; "Are blacks better: on sport's last taboo" by Malcolm Gladwell, *The New Yorker*, May 19, 1997; "What Ever Happened to the White Athlete" by S.L. Price, *Sports Illustrated*, December 8, 1997; "Athletes' egos drawn in black and white" by Jan Wong, *Globe and Mail*, December 13, 1997. One of those Black citizens stopped for no apparent reason was Canadian heavyweight boxer Kirk Johnson whose car was seized, leaving him stranded on the side of a highway in 1998 and for which he received a formal apology as reported by Canadian Press "Johnson receives police apology; Chief admits to discrimination," January 20, 2004; "The Anatomy of Scientific Racism: Racialist Responses to Black Athletic Achievement" by Patrick B. Miller, *The Journal of Sport History*, Vol. 25, No. 1, Spring 1988.

PART TWO

3: CANADA'S EARLY YEARS

Accounts about Major Taylor include www.majortaylorassociation.org; *Major Taylor* by Andrew Ritchie (San Francisco: Bicycle Books, 1988); and *The Fastest Bicycle Rider in the World* by Major Taylor (Worcester: Wormley Publishing, 1928). The extraordinary story of Robert Berry awaits additional research, but the essence of his banishment from the Toronto Regatta in the months following Confederation can be found in the *Toronto Globe* on August 9, 12, 13, 1867; other background on Berry and 19th century rowing in Canada included *Historical Sketch of the Argonaut Rowing Club, 1872 to 1911* (Toronto: 1911); *Rowing in Canada Since 1848* by Robert S. Hunter's (Hamilton: David-Lisson, 1933); and *More than an Island: A History of the Toronto Island* by Sally Gibson (Toronto: Irwin, 1984). The 1802 account of a Black child in a skiff appears in *The Town of York 1793–1815: A Collection of Documents of Early Toronto*, edited by Edith Firth (Toronto: University of Toronto Press, 1962). Early writing by the author on this topic appeared in *Horizon Canada*, Volume 2, Number 22, July 1985 under "Black athletes have a long history of participation in Canadian sporting life." See also "British Officials and Their Attitudes to the Negro Community in Canada, 1833–1861" by Ged Martin, *Ontario History*, June 1974.

4: LOOKING OUTSIDE CANADA FOR OPPORTUNITY

In *The Moveable Feast*, Ernest Hemingway, writing about his time in Paris in the 1920s, said, "There is no mention of the Stade Anastasie where the boxers served as waiters at the tables set out under the trees and the ring was the garden. Nor of training with Larry Gains, nor the great twenty-round fights at the Cirque d'Hiver ... It would be fine if all these were in this book but we will have to do without them for now." *The Impossible Dream* by Larry Gains (London: Leisure Publications, n.d.) provided background, while some of the best material on Larry Gains came about during my participation in the

British Sports History Conference in Liverpool, U.K., in 2000 and a presentation on "The Abolition of the Colour Bar in British Boxing" by Gary Shaw. Two significant histories of boxing in Canada are *Goin' The Distance: Canada's Boxing Heritage* by Murray Greig (Toronto: Macmillan, 1996), and *Tommy Burns: Canada's Unknown World Heavyweight Champion* by Dan McCaffery (Toronto: James Lorimer, 2000). also helpful was an excerpt from Dr. Alexander Young Jr.'s manuscript on Sam Langford, "The Boston Tarbaby" *Nova Scotia Historical Quarterly*, Vol. 4, No. 3 (1974).

5: BLACK BASEBALL'S EARLY DAYS IN CANADA

Sources on the Black experience in Montreal include: *The Road to Now: A History of the Blacks in Montreal* (Montreal: Véhicule Press, 1997) and *Jackie Robinson: A Biography* by Arnold Rampersad (New York: Knopf, 1997). Other sources for this chapter include: "'34 legends the class of '00" by Mark Malone, *Chatham Daily News*, September 2, 2000 and "Those All-Star seasons" by Dave Feschuk, *National Post*, July 13, 2002, stories on the Chatham Colored All-Stars; *Globe*, October 16, 23, 24, 1934, original information on the Chatham-Penetang series of 1934; "A Shameful Day in the Annals of Canadian Baseball" by Dan Ziniuk, *Ottawa Citizen*, June 21, 1998, the account of the summer of 1936 All-Star game in which Black players in the Quebec Provincial League were refused the opportunity to play; correspondence from E.G. Hastings of Dunnville, Ontario, April 30, 1984, January 29, 1984 and February 22, 1985; "Baseball once the 'Big' sport in Dunnville" by E.G. Hastings, *Dunnville Chronicle*, August 31, 1977; telephone interviews with former Negro League player Jimmy Wilkes and Lorraine Clifford, wife of former Negro League player Shanty Clifford, both in 1987; "Our greatest athlete, Ollie Johnson, dies," *Oakville Beaver*, February 9, 1977; *The Great American Sports Book* by George Gipe (New York: Doubleday, 1978), 316 for the item on Tip O'Neill's refusal to play against a Black baseball team; *Chicago Defender*, editorial, April 13, 1946, on the irony of the first two Negroes in baseball having to play in Canada; and in *Canadian Living*, June 1995, Laura Bickle's story on J.J. Evans.

6: SPORTING IMMIGRANTS AND THEIR DESCENDANTS

The Canadian Rodeo Book by Claire Eamer and Thirza Jones (Saskatoon: Western Producer Prairie Books, 1982) for information on John Ware; "One man reclamation project" (about Lew Hayman) in the Toronto Argonauts' program *CFL Illustrated*, September 1979, describes the Herb

Trawick incident; and "First black opposing player unsettled Argonaut officials" by Jim Proudfoot, *Toronto Star*, September 27, 1997.

7: RUNNING FOR CANADA

My research on these missing years of track and field history included interviews with Sam Richardson in the early 1980s, when he was my guest at Seneca College, and later, by telephone, with Ray Lewis. James Worrall, of the Canadian Olympic Association, Edwards' daughter, Gwen Emery, of Alert Bay, British Columbia, and his sister, Sarah Grey, of New York City, provided personal information on Phil Edwards.

8: LONELY YEARS OF ACHIEVEMENT

Stories on Earl Walls include: "Earl Walls a giant of the ring" by Norman Da Costa, *Toronto Star*, December 16, 1996, and "Lives Lived—Earl Walls" by Stephen Brunt, *Globe and Mail*, January 1, 1997; material on Fred Thomas provided by Tony Techko of the Windsor-Essex County Sports Hall of Fame and Museum, including "Fred Thomas" by Tony Techko, *Windsor This Month*, May 1981.

9: IMMIGRATION'S GREAT REWARDS

Stories on Donovan Bailey include: "Bailey playing his usual games" by Steve Buffery, *London Free Press*, July 24, 1997, and a student submission in my sports history class at Seneca College on Donovan Bailey by Phyllis Opoku-Mensah, June 26, 1997. Material on Molly Killingbeck came from the Windsor Sports Hall of Fame, including "Speed Merchant" by Dave Hall, *Windsor Star* Commonwealth Games '94 preview.

10: THE FRUITS OF STRUGGLE

"Canadian hoop star gives something back to school" by David Grossman, *Toronto Star*, October 9, 1997, a story on Sue Stewart. I have written extensively on Ferguson Jenkins in my books on baseball including, *Diamonds of the North: A Concise History of Baseball in Canada* (Toronto: Oxford University Press, 1995).

11: HOCKEY: THE CANADIAN SPECIFIC

Angela James' story is told in *Black Tights: Women, Sport and Sexuality* by Laura Robinson (Toronto: Harper Collins, 2002). Personal information and articles on the all-Black hockey team of St. Catharines were provided by Donna Ford, whose father Richard Nicholson played for the team. Other sources for this chapter include: *The Puck Stops Here* by Garth Vaughan (Fredericton: Goose Lane, 1996), for information on the Colored Hockey league; "Hockey's Black Story" by Michael McKinley, *National Post*, February 27, 1999; "More than the puck is black" by Michael Clarkson, *Toronto Star*, December 19, 2003; *Breaking the Ice: The Black Experience in Professional Hockey* by Cecil Harris (Toronto: Insomniac Press, 2003); "Jarome Iginla—Making History in the NHL" by Jo Ann Lawery from www.blackathlete.com; "Black in Blue" by Joe O'Connor, *National Post*, September 13, 2003, on Rane Carnegie's chance to play for the Maple Leafs; stories on Herb Carnegie, include "Colour bar shattered one Canadian's NHL dream" by James Christie, *Globe and Mail*, April 5, 1997, "Color bar kept Carnegie from NHL career" by Jim Proudfoot, *Toronto Star*, July 30, 1997, and *A Fly in a Pail of Milk* by Herb Carnegie (Oakville: Mosaic Press, 1997), his autobiography; "Mike Grier" (profile) *Official*, magazine of the Edmonton Oilers, November 27, 1996; "Anson Carter" (profile) by Damien Cox, *Canadian Hockey Magazine* (1997/98 Edition); "Willie O'Ree: King of the Near-Miss" by Bill Libby, *Hockey Pictorial*, December 1964; "Londoner Hits "Big Time" Hockey Fifty Years After Missing Chance" by Ernie Miller, April 20, 1963, (unreferenced story, possibly from *London Free Press*); "Coloured Hockey Players" *Woodstock Sentinel Review*, February 2, 1899, on Galloway and Lightfoot; "On thin ice" by Randy Starkman, *Toronto Star*, November 23, 1997, a story about former NHLer Mike Marson; "Simon's sentence market driven" by Mark Zwolinski, *Toronto Star*, November 12, 1997, a description of Chris Simon's suspension; "Racial abuse on rise in MTHL, black referee says" by Lois Kalchman, *Toronto Star*, November 11, 1997; *Echoes in the Rink* (review) by William Houston, *Globe and Mail*, December 27, 1997 documentary about Willie O'Ree and his fight with Eric Nesterenko.

12: VISITING HEROES

The visitors who remained in Canada include: "Crazy Legs put a stiff arm on racism" by James Christie, *Globe and Mail*, recalling the Ulysses Curtis story; "Ex-CFLers honoured" by Michael Clarkson, *Toronto Star*, February 4, 2004; "Their loss, our gain" by Ron Haggart, *Globe and Mail*, October 13, 2003, Black American quarterbacks who came to Canada because they couldn't play their position in the National Football League; *Sizing Up Mr. Big* by David Berman, *Canadian Business*, June 1997, on

Isiah Thomas; *Slam Dunk: The Raptors and the NBA in Canada* by Brendan Connor and Nancy Russell, (Toronto: Prentice Hall, 1995).

I was introduced to the sports experience of new Canadian citizens in my sports history class at Seneca College and these included essays by Abdullahi Hersi, "Sport History of the Somali Canadian Community," June 27, 2000, Kuri Tesfaye, "Ethio-Stars Sports Club of Toronto," April 1, 2000, Francis Freddy, "Cambridge Cricket Club" (no date); Mustafa Ismail, "Somali United Soccer Club," April 11, 2000, and Mohamed Abdalla, "Muslim Soccer League in Toronto" (no date). Accounts of the BigUp Volleyball team were based on interviews with Shondell Brooks, Marc Roberts and Roland Lewis as part of the background for a story in *True North* magazine and background for the BigUp name from the song "Black Trump" from the *Rude Awakening* album by artist Cocoa Brovaz. Daniel Igali's story is told on his web site, www.igali.com. Background on Canada's national cricket team is available by "googling" the Canadian Cricket Association. Other sources for this chapter include: *National Post*, January 2, 2004, information on Toronto homicides in 2003; "Discovering Perdita" by Sean Fitz-Gerald, *National Post*, December 29, 2003, and "Still the same old Perdita" by Randy Starkman, *Toronto Star*, October 5, 2003, for stories on Perdita Felicien; www.barbadosturfclub.com and www.woodbineentertainment.com for stories on Patrick Husbands; "Canadians met with hostility abroad" by Norman Da Costa, *Toronto Star*, October 11, 1997, the experience in Germany of soccer players Jason Bent and Dwayne de Rosario; *Lexington Herald-Leader's* College Basketball Special Edition (November 16, 1997) recorded Jamaal Magloire's comments on returning to Toronto.

Index

About the Author

A Sporting Chance follows in a line of groundbreaking stories written by William Humber about Canada's sports past,including histories of baseball and bicycling in Canada. Acknowledged on their broadcasts, as one of Canada's leading sports historians, by among others the CBC, TV Ontario and TSN, he has spoken at sports history conferences in the United States and the United Kingdom as well as in Canada. Bill has taught a credit subject on Canadian sports history for the last ten years at Seneca College in Toronto where he is the chair of the college's Centre for the Built Environment, a North American leader in providing education on urban sustainability for technologists.

Humber is a selector for Canada's Sports Hall of Fame, Canada's Baseball Hall of Fame, as well as his hometown Clarington Sports Hall of Fame, and was an honorary inductee into Saskatchewan's Baseball Hall of Fame in 2004. He is included in the *Canadian Who's Who*, was a recipient of a Queen's Golden Jubilee medal in 2003, and lives with his family in Bowmanville, Ontario, where he is active in many aspects of his community's character and future growth.

This is Humber's tenth book and second with Natural Heritage Books, his first being *Bowmanville: A Small Town at the Edge* (1997).